Assertive Discipline

A Take Charge Approach For Today's Educator

Lee Canter
and
Marlene Canter

A Publication of Lee Canter & Associates

To John Nicholson—his firm limits and positive warmth and support made this book possible. He truly was "The" Assertive Teacher!

© 1976 Lee Canter & Associates
P.O. Box 2113, Santa Monica, CA 90406
(800) 262-4347   (213) 395-3221

Printed in the United States of America

L.C. No. 76-42182
ISBN 0-9608978-0-1

First printing 1976; Twenty-seventh printing April 1990

ACKNOWLEDGEMENTS

Our deepest thanks to all those who made this book possible. Terry Paulson, Assertion Training Institute, he helped get the ball rolling. The staffs of Oceanview and Irvine School Districts, their openness and support helped the word get around. Gene Bedley, El Camino Real School, Irvine, "The" Assertive Principal; Sue Coleman, the editor; Lois English, the typist; and finally to all the teachers we have trained. You have believed in us and our ideas. Your feedback and support have kept us going. You have made it all worth while.

We thank you all!

Contents

Introduction   v
I. Power To The Teacher   1
II. Discriminating Response Styles   15
III. Roadblocks To Assertive Discipline   45
IV. Your Wants and Needs: What Are They?
How Do You Get Them Met?   61
V. Verbal Limit-Setting   71
VI. Limit-Setting Follow-Through:
A Promise Not A Threat   91
VII. Positive Assertion: Verbal And
Follow-Through   117
VIII. But, What If They All Do It?—Assertive
Classroom Management Skills   135
IX. The Assertive Discipline Plan And Other
Persistency Building Procedures   145
X. Asking For Help: The Use of Assertive
Skills With Parents and Principals   155
XI. In Conclusion: Assertive Discipline
Comes Down To the Issue of Choice   173
Assertive Discipline Worksheets   179

INTRODUCTION

Assertive Discipline is an outgrowth of our professional efforts in working directly with children with behavior problems and consulting with classroom teachers on how to deal effectively with such children.

Assertive Discipline resulted primarily from our exposure to the theoretical and practical aspects of *Assertion Training*. *Assertion Training* is a systematic approach designed to help individuals learn more effectively to express their wants and feelings, a means for increasing their ability to get their needs met in both personal and professional relationships. The use of *Assertion Training* skills enables individuals to stand up more effectively for their wants and feelings, while at the same time not abusing the rights of others. These skills are designed to enable an individual to develop as much positive influence in relationships as is possible. In clinical practice, professionals have successfully used *Assertion Training* skills to assist a wide spectrum of individuals: from businessmen to adolescents; to housewives; to patients in hospitals; to overwhelmed parents.

In *Assertion Training* the focus is on three general response styles of individuals: *non-assertive, assertive,* and *hostile*. A non-assertive response style, also known as passive or "wishy-washy," is one by which individuals do not clearly express their wants or feelings, nor do they back up their words with the necessary positive action. A hostile response style is one by which individuals express their personal wants and feelings, but in a way that "puts down" others, or abuses their rights. By contrast, an assertive response is one by which individuals express their wants and feelings, and back them up with positive actions if necessary.

While consulting with teachers, we were constantly struck by how overwhelmed and "powerless" many of them felt to deal with the behavior problems in their classrooms. As we observed more and more teachers in their classrooms, we became aware that many of them lacked the skills and confidence to set down assertively the limits they wanted and follow through if the children did or did not respond to what they demanded. We became cognizant of how so many teachers were either non-assertive and allowed the children to take advantage of them, or hostile and "put down" the children to make them behave.

As a result of our observations we decided to try an experiment. We included some basic *Assertion Training* skills in our on-going courses for teachers. The response was overwhelming. The teachers quickly learned and successfully applied the skills in their classrooms, to the benefit of both themselves and the children. As the course progressed the teachers became assertive with us, and asked us to provide them with more and more *Assertive Training* skills. The teachers' positive response gave us the incentive to modify further *Assertion Training* skills to meet the special needs of classroom teachers: *Assertive Discipline* was the result.

The response to *Assertive Discipline* by the educational community has been phenomenal. We have been asked to offer countless workshops throughout California. In no way can we or our staff meet the needs of teachers interested in learning about *Assertive Discipline*. Thus, we designed this book to assist the classroom teacher in learning and implementing *Assertive Discipline* skills in her* classroom.

*Unfortunately, the English language does not yet have a third person, singular pronoun applicable to both sexes. Therefore, we refer to all teachers as "she" and to all students as "he."

POWER TO THE
TEACHER

You, the teacher, must be able to get your needs met in the classroom. You have needs, wants and feelings just like the children in your classroom. You can need a quiet classroom as much as a child can need to talk and make noise. You can want the child to stay in his seat as much as the child can want to wander around the room. You can feel as terrible at the end of a conflict-"hassle"-ridden day as can the child. If you need a quiet class to teach effectively, you have the right to ask for quiet. If you want the children to stay in their seats during work time, you have the right to ask for it! If you want respect from the children, you have the right to ask them not to talk back to you! It is only when a teacher takes seriously her own needs, wants and feelings that she will be in a position to feel good about herself as an individual and as a teacher.

We feel that your needs will be met when you implement these following "rights":

1. The right to establish a classroom structure and routine that provides the optimal learning environment in light of your own strengths and weaknesses.

2. The right to determine and request appropriate behavior from the students which meet your needs and encourage the positive social and educational development of the child.

3. The right to ask for help from parents, the principal, etc., when you need assistance with a child.

In order to get your needs met, you must be in the position to influence the behavior of the children. How can you get the quiet you need, if you can't get the children to stop talking? How can you get the children to stay in their seats, if they will not listen to you? How can you get the respect you want, if you can't get the children to stop talking back? Without influence you are "powerless" and will become "burned out," etc.

Why is it that so many teachers are having difficulty with their students and are feeling "powerless," depressed, embittered, burned out? What's happened? There is no simple answer. A number of complex factors have combined to create an environment in which teachers are encountering greater difficulty in getting their personal and professional needs met.

The role status of the contemporary teacher, as with any authority figure in society, be it law officer, doctor or even President, has declined in recent years. Up until a few years ago, the teacher was viewed in "awe" by both students and their parents. The teacher, simply because of her role status, had respect and authority. Thus, she was a very "powerful" figure in the eyes of the students and could easily influence the students' behavior, often with just a look, a smile, or a threat.

All of that is now changed, more, of course, in some areas than in others. Today, a teacher has to *earn* the respect of both students and their parents. Children, especially in the upper grades, do not hold their teacher in the "awe" they used to. Often, a teacher's look, smile, or threat is simply disregarded by such students. In reality, the teacher's basic techniques of influence (discipline) are no longer as effective in getting the desired results. The discipline approaches of the 1950's and 1960's do not work with the students of the 1970's.

In addition, the teacher cannot rely upon the unending support of all the students' parents. Many parents are openly questioning, sometimes with justification, the education that their children are receiving, and do not feel they want to support the wants or needs of their child's teachers.

The changes in the students' and parents' perceptions of the role status of teachers have been paralleled by changes in how teachers view themselves. It is no longer fashionable to be the "rigid, authoritarian, traditional, disciplinarian" of bygone days. Instead, psychology, namely the philosophies of Doctors Freud, Skinner (Behavior Modification), Glasser (*Schools Without Failure*), and Gordon (*P.E.T.* and *Teacher Effectiveness Training*) has been brought into the classroom. These philosophies of discipline have had a major impact upon contemporary teachers. The problem is that these ideas have often been *distorted* and misinterpreted to the point that teachers have been led to believe fallacies such as:

If you discipline a child you will cause him irreparable "psychic trauma."

Avoid all conflict with the child. If a child is "ripping apart" the classroom, don't confront him, find him an alternative activity that will better meet his needs.

Teachers *must* understand the causes of a child's problem behavior. The child may be driven by "unconscious" drives and cannot control his "neurotic" behavior.

In order to get a child to behave, all a teacher needs to do is feed him full of M&M's when he is good, and ignore him when he is bad.

When a child is upset and disruptive, you need to help him express his feelings before you can get him to behave.

As a result of being exposed to so many philosophies, teachers tend to question constantly how they discipline their students: "Was I too hard on Mark?" "Should I have used 'Behavior Mod' before I called his mom?" "Should I be so strict with Steve because he has such emotional problems?" Guilt, anxiety, and frustration are the result of such questioning. You cannot get your needs met in your classroom unless you have an effective method of discipline which you thoroughly understand and are comfortable utilizing.

The basic foundations of educational philosophy have changed along with the theories of discipline. There is no longer just *one way* to run a classroom and teach students. In the past most teachers placed the same basic expectations on all children. They expected the child to sit in his seat, work without talking, raise his hand, work at his desk, do the work he was told to do and when he was told to do it. Today, expectations may vary greatly from teacher to teacher. They may range from the previously mentioned expectations of more "traditional" teachers to those of more "open structured" teachers. These teachers may allow the children to talk all they want, work wherever they want (on the rug, pillows, etc.), get up whenever they feel like it, even choose which assignments they want to do and when they want to do them.

Such a variance in expectations among teachers naturally produces fewer and less clear-cut standards of acceptable behavior as compared to the standards of the past. This often results in a child's statement of "My other teacher didn't make me do that, it's not fair," or "Why can't I do it like I did in my other class?" Thus, a teacher today will not only have greater difficulty in determining her own wants and needs, but in establishing and communicating these expectancies to children who may be accustomed to a variety of standards set by other teachers.

Regardless of varying expectancies, statistics clearly indicate that the perceptions of veteran teachers are highly valid: There are more children, with more behavior problems, in the public schools than ever before. Why this is so, we really don't know. What we do know is that, first, classroom teachers are required to work with these children, and that, second, most of these teachers have had *NO* training in how to interact with such students. Most teachers have only been trained in how to teach "nice, normal children," with no emotional, behavioral, physical, or learning problems. As one teacher told us: "If you are lucky, you have 3 or 4 such 'normal' children in your class. Don't ask me how to deal with the other 30!" This means that teachers are called upon to perform a function in which they have had no training, for it takes specific skills and confidence to deal with children with behavioral and emotional problems.

Today's teachers must contend with one other factor. We call it the "Myth of the Good Teacher." This myth basically goes as follows: "A 'good' teacher should be able to handle all behavior problems on her own, and within the confines of the classroom." This means, if you are competent, you should never need to go to your principal or the child's parents for assistance. This myth began many years ago when the factors that we have discussed did not exist. No one teacher, no matter how good she is, or how much experience or training she has, is capable of working successfully with each and every child without support. There are many students today whose behavior is so disruptive that a teacher must have assistance from both the principal and the parent(s) in order to deal effectively with the child and his behavior.

This "myth" places a burden of guilt upon teachers who encounter problems with their students. According to the myth, if they were "really good" they wouldn't have these problems. These guilt-ridden, inadequate feelings tend to keep teachers from asking for the help they need with certain students.

The various factors of lowered role status, conflicting professional philosophies, increasing numbers of problem students, lack of training, and unrealistic expectations, have combined to diminish a teacher's real and perceived ability to influence the students' behaviors. Without this influence the teacher again will be unable to meet her needs. The lack of influence also hinders the teacher's ability to meet the needs of the students.

In order to grow educationally, socially, and emotionally, children need to be in an environment in which there is a concerned teacher who will set firm, consistent, positive limits while providing warmth and support for their appropriate behavior. We have all seen the effects on children who come from a home in which the parents are not concerned enough to set firm limits with them; "Little Monsters," "Brats," etc., are the result. When children do not have the limits they need, they will "act up" in order to make the adults around them take notice. A child's inappropriate behavior is often a plea by the child for someone, i.e., the teacher, to care enough about him to make him stop.

Without consistent, firm, positive limits in the classroom, children will fear for their emotional, and yes, even physical safety. Children need to know what response there will be to their behavior by the teacher, both positive and negative. It is only then that the child will be in the position to *choose* how he will behave.

Concurrent with the setting of limits, you, the teacher, need to be in a position to provide the child with warmth and support. All children need "strokes" to let them know that they and their positive behaviors are appreciated. The child needs to know you will recognize and support his positive behavior just as you will limit his inappropriate behavior. Trust and respect are established in a relationship in which the child knows he will get honest feedback from you: "I like when you do this," or, "I don't like it when you do that."

We believe the child has the right to:

1. Have a teacher who is in a position to and will help the child limit his inappropriate self-disruptive behavior,

2. Have a teacher who is in the position to and will provide the child with positive support for his appropriate behavior, and

3. Choose how to behave and know the consequences that will follow.

For a teacher to be in the position to meet these rights (needs) of the children, she again must have influence. Without influence, how can she set the limits for the child? Without influence, how can she provide support for the child? Without influence, how can she provide meaningful consequences for behavior?

Given the aforementioned realities of contemporary

teachers, the questions which naturally evolve focus on how these teachers can increase their influence with their students. How do they establish their rights? How do they get their wants and needs met? How do they meet the wants and needs of their students? We thus come to the goal of *Assertive Discipline,* this goal being to help teachers increase their influence in their classroom by becoming more *assertive.*

What do we mean by *assertive?* Webster's Dictionary defines the verb "assert" as: "To state or affirm positively, assuredly, plainly, or strongly." For our purposes we define an assertive teacher as: *"One who clearly and firmly communicates her wants and needs to her students, and is prepared to reinforce her words with appropriate actions. She responds in a manner which maximizes her potential to get her needs met, but in no way violates the best interests of the students."*

How will being assertive help you, the teacher, influence the behavior of students? When a teacher is assertive, and clearly and firmly communicates her wants and feelings to a child, she sends a very clear message. This message says: "I care too much about myself to allow you to take advantage of my wants or feelings! I care too much to allow you to act in an inappropriate manner without my responding! I, as well, care too much about you to allow your inappropriate behavior to go unnoticed by me!" Simply stated, the assertive teacher lets the child know that she means what she says and says what she means!

By being assertive a teacher establishes the *parameters* of what she expects from the child and what the child can expect in return from the teacher. These parameters of the teacher's "wants" and the "consequences" serve to maximize the potential positive influence she can have on the child and his behavior.

Assertive Discipline is based upon the reality of potential, positive influence that teachers can have on the behavior of their students. Through *Assertive Discipline* teachers can learn to "take charge" of their classroom in a firm, yet positive manner. This approach does not advocate teachers storming into their classroom and "throttling" any student who opens his mouth. What it does advocate is that teachers need to set firm, consistent limits, while at the same time remaining cognizant of the students' needs for warmth and positive support.

Assertive Discipline is designed to provide the teacher with the skills and confidence necessary to help her to (1) identify her wants and needs, (2) identify her personal "roadblocks" to getting her wants and needs met, and (3) to learn how cognitively and behaviorally to overcome these "roadblocks" in order to maximize her assertive potential.

Assertive Discipline is based primarily upon the principles of Assertion Training which has evolved from social learning theory research. Assertion Training skills, therefore, have been developed by professionals who have conducted extensive research in the area of interpersonal communication. Among the skill factors identified were an individual's ability to: (1) identify wants and feelings in interpersonal situations; (2) verbalize wants and feelings both positive, "I like that," and negative, "I don't like that"; (3) persist in stating wants and feelings; (4) verbalize in a firm tone of voice; (5) maintain eye contact when speaking; and (6) reinforce verbal statements with congruent non-verbal gestures.

More importantly, Assertion Training professionals

have developed effective cognitive and behavioral methods of training individuals in order to increase their interpersonal skills. Assertion Training Groups and workshops
have sprung up throughout the country. Through such
encounters, individuals have been helped to increase
their skills and confidence in dealing with interpersonal
situations as:

Refusing a request: Being able to say "no" to requests
that they do not want to do, without feeling guilty.

Giving or receiving a compliment: Expressing a sincere
statement of a positive feeling, be it warmth, apprecia-
tion, or concern.

Expressing negative interpersonal feedback: Expressing
a thought or feeling that might intimidate others.

Standing up for their rights "under fire": Sticking to
their wants or feelings even when criticized or challenged
by others.

Placing demands on others: Comfortably being able to
make a request of others.

The Assertion Training movement has been spurred by
such well-received books as Manual Smith's *When I Say
No I Feel Guilty*, Robert Alberti and Michael Emmons'
Your Perfect Right, and Stanlee Philips and Nancy Austins'
The Assertive Woman.

In *Assertive Discipline* we have adapted the previous
principles and skills of *Assertion Training* to meet the
unique needs of the classroom teacher. How, then, can
the use of *Assertive Discipline* be beneficial for a teacher?

Assertive Discipline can help the teacher identify situations in which she needs to be assertive for her benefit and the benefit of the child.

Assertive Discipline can help the teacher to develop more consistent and effective communication with her students. It can help her to know when and how to set limits verbally, as well as when and how to provide the children the verbal praise and support they need.

Assertive Discipline can help the "passive, inconsistent" teacher gain the confidence and skills to become firmer and more consistent in her demands of her students.

Assertive Discipline can help the "hostile, angry" teacher learn to influence the students' behavior without constant yelling and vague, unrealistic threats.

Assertive Discipline can help the "negative" teacher learn how to use her "positive" influence on the behavior of her students.

Assertive Discipline can help the "overwhelmed" teacher gain the confidence and learn the skills necessary to gain the influence she needs to help the children learn the appropriate behavior in the classroom.

Assertive Discipline can provide any teacher the *confidence* and *skills* necessary to help her work more successfully with "the Behavior Problem" in her class she has been unable to get through to.

Assertive Discipline is not a "cure-all" for any and all problems that develop in the classroom. We don't feel that a "cure-all" exists. Thus, before we progress it is only fair that we spell out some "Words of Caution."

Assertive Discipline will not and cannot give a teacher a fool-proof way always to "be successful." A teacher cannot make all her students become model students; they still have the right to choose not to learn or to misbehave, in spite of all your efforts. *Assertive Discipline* only helps a teacher take an active stance towards doing what she can to influence the behavior of her students.

Assertive Discipline will not provide a teacher with a "blueprint" for every difficult classroom problem. We do not expect the "techniques" or "approaches" to be seen as the "only way" or the "right way" to handle all situations; they are only options that a teacher can choose to make part of her personal repertoire. This book is not meant to be another "should," but an exploration of some of the available options.

Therefore, the chapters that follow will:

1. Discriminate between the effective and ineffective response styles of teachers.

2. Explain how teachers set up personal "roadblocks" to their becoming assertive.

3. Explain how a teacher can identify her wants and needs in the classroom.

4. Describe cognitive and behavioral procedures which can help a teacher change her ineffective response styles.

5. Describe the skills a teacher needs to express verbally her wants and feelings.

6. Describe the skills a teacher needs to follow through on her verbal responses.

7. Describe persistency building procedures designed to assist a teacher in establishing consistently assertive responses.

8. Describe how teachers can clearly and firmly express their wants and feelings with parents and principals.

2

DISCRIMINATING
RESPONSE STYLES

In beginning any discussion of *Assertive Discipline,* we need to start with a description of the three basic response styles teachers utilize in their interactions with their students. The response styles are *non-assertive, assertive,* and *hostile.*

A *non-assertive* response style is one in which the teacher does not clearly let the child know what she wants or if she does, she doesn't stand up for what she wants by backing up her words with appropriate actions. Such a "passive" response style is illustrated by the following example of a teacher attempting to set limits with her students.

> Ms. W. is a second-year teacher with a 6th grade class. She is still unsure of herself and her abilities. There are many days she feels basically "powerless" to deal with behavior of some of her students. Her students are well aware of her insecurities, and certain students take advantage of her whenever they can. One particular problem she has is that a small group of children are constantly out of their seats talking with one another during work time. During a math lesson we observed Ms. W. looking disconcertedly at three students who were out of their seats and talking by the pencil sharpener. For several minutes she allowed the children to talk and finally walked up to them and asked them to "please try" to sit down and get to work. The students said they would as soon as they finished sharpening their pencils. Five minutes later they were still there and she again went up to them, this time stating, "I just don't know what to do with you kids. If you don't do your work that's your problem. I give up with you!" The children started toward their seats, but got side-tracked talking to another child whose seat was on the way. In frustration Ms. W. threw her hands up in the air and just shook her head. When we spoke with her

about the situation after class she stated, "I've learned it doesn't work to get on the children, they are impossible kids who really don't listen to what I say anyway. I'm so frustrated with this class I could just scream!"

A *hostile* response style is one in which the teacher expresses her wants and feelings, but in a manner which abuses the rights or feelings of the children. Such a "negative" response style is illustrated by the following example of a teacher's limit-setting attempts.

Mr. T. is a 5th grade teacher. He believes the only way to get children to behave is with "iron-fisted" discipline. To say the least, he believes in being tough on the children "for their own good." His new class has been particularly difficult for him. He has several students who have had a history of defying teachers. One of them, Michael, was disruptive the day we observed. During the class discussion, Michael would continuously poke his neighbors and make fun of those children who were responding to Mr. T.'s questions. Upon observing Michael's behavior, Mr. T. walked over to him, grabbed him by the arm and shouted, "I've had it with you, young man. If you act like a 'fool,' I'll treat you like one. If I catch you acting that way again, you will be sorry you ever were in my class." Several of the children sitting by Michael began to giggle as Mr. T. berated Michael. Michael sat there fuming, plotting how he would get back at the teacher and the children who had laughed at him. When we spoke with Mr. T., he shared that he didn't like getting so angry with Michael, but that he just didn't know what else to do with him.

An *assertive* response style is one in which the teacher clearly communicates her wants and feelings to the students and is prepared to back up her words with appropriate actions. The response is planned to maximize the teacher's potential to get her needs met without violating the best interest of the students. When a teacher responds assertively to a child's inappropriate behavior, it is called *assertive limit setting.* This is illustrated by the teacher in the following example.

> Ms. L. was a 1st grade teacher. She was a skilled and confident professional. She believed children needed firm, positive limits and was prepared to do what she could to help set such limits in her class. There were several children in her class who had difficulty controlling their aggressive behavior, Paul being a particular problem. When we were present, Paul was upset and began to hit a boy he was playing with. Ms. L. went up to Paul and firmly told him, "Paul, stop fighting!" She continued with, "Paul, I will not tolerate your fighting. You have a choice, either stop fighting in this class, or I will send you to the corner whenever you fight." Paul began to protest, "I don't want to go to the corner." Ms. L. responded, "Then you will have to control your temper and not fight." Paul was well behaved and played cooperatively the rest of the day. In our conversation with Ms. L., she emphasized that she did not like to discipline children, but she knew they needed the limits only she could provide in the classroom. She concluded, "Paul knew I meant what I said. I have sent other children to the corner when they needed it, and I would send him too."

A teacher also can react to a child's appropriate (positive) behavior with a non-assertive, hostile, or assertive response style. When the students do what the teacher wants and the teacher ignores them or does not clearly communicate her pleasure to the students, the response is non-assertive. A classic illustration would be:

> Mr. L. was a veteran 8th grade math teacher. He had a good deal of difficulty getting the students to pay attention in class. He was constantly reprimanding students when they were not paying attention; but when we observed we noted that he would rarely, if ever, respond in a positive manner to those students who did pay attention as he asked. When we asked him about why he basically "ignored" those students who did what he wanted, he said, "Students are just supposed to be 'good' without prompting from the teacher."

When the students do what the teacher wants, and the teacher comments in a negative, sarcastic, or degrading manner, this is a hostile response. Here is an example of what we mean.

> Ms. R. taught 4th grade. She had to spend a good deal of her time dealing with discipline problems, especially those of Mark, an extremely disruptive child who would constantly shout out during class. Mark's outbursts frustrated her to no end and caused her naturally to feel a good deal of hostility towards him. On the day we observed, Mark was quiet for the first half hour we were there. When Ms. R. became aware of the lack of Mark's outbursts, she sarcastically remarked to him, "It's about time you acted your age and controlled your mouth!" Within five minutes Mark's mouth was going more than ever.

An assertive response to desired behavior is one in which the teacher clearly communicates to the child her positive recognition of and support for the behavior. We call assertive responses in support of appropriate behavior, *positive assertions*. Here is an excellent example.

> Mr. K. taught 6th grade at an inner city school. He had a tough class. His main problem was getting the students to complete their assignments. Worst of all was Raul, who spent more time disrupting than working. The day we were in his class Raul completed his assignments. Mr. K. enthusiastically let Raul know he liked what he had done, "Out of sight job, Raul." He added, "You did such a fine job today, I'm going to send a note home to your folks letting them know how pleased I am." Raul beamed, for the only notes his parents had ever received previously were on those occasions when he had been "bad."

Before we continue further, we need to make an important point: *No teacher responds in the same manner all of the time. Therefore, no teacher is assertive all of the time. No teacher is non-assertive all of the time. And, no teacher is hostile all of the time.* All teachers respond differently at different times. On a "good day" you may be more assertive; on a "tired day" more non-assertive; on a "bad day" more hostile. It is our goal to help you to establish more consistently assertive responses on "all days." In order for us to do this, we need to elaborate on the different response styles so that you can easily identify when you are employing a particular style.

NON-ASSERTIVE

When a teacher responds non-assertively, she does not clearly make her needs or wants known to the children. She will allow the children to take advantage of her without firmly responding to the situation. She will often be "wishy-washy" in her demands to the children, and appear to be unsure of herself and her abilities. She will communicate to the children, "I'm afraid of you. I feel 'powerless' to deal with you." In general, the teacher will take a "passive" posture in the classroom, providing neither positive limits nor positive support.

Let's elaborate on these generalities about non-assertive teachers. When confronted with a child's inappropriate behavior, which needs to be responded to with a firm request to "stop" and/or an appropriate follow-through action, a non-assertive teacher may do any of the following; (the first two examples are based upon the theoretical work of Randell Foster, M.D.).

1. Ask the child to accomplish an intermediate behavior goal. For example, after breaking up a fight provoked by a child who constantly engages in physical aggression, instead of demanding he "stop fighting in school," the teacher may:

Ask child to make an effort to change: "I want you to really *try* to stop fighting."

Ask child to think about his behavior: "You had better start thinking about things before you just start swinging."

Ask child to improve his behavior: "I want you to try to cut down on the number of fights you have at school."

Ask child to be concerned about behavior: "You had better start feeling bad about how you pick on your classmates."

Ask child not to get caught at behavior: "You had better never let me *catch* you fighting again."

Ask child to learn appropriate behavior: "It's about time you learn fighting is not the right way to settle your problems."

Ask child to discuss reason(s) for his behavior: "I want you to tell me why you fight all the time."

Ask child to face up to problem behavior: "You had better face that you have a problem with all this fighting you do."

Ask child to accept help: "I want you to let me or someone else help you with your fighting problem."

If you note, the intermediate goals are well-intentioned, but they in no way communicate to the child what the teacher really wants him to do, that is, stop fighting.

2. Make a statement, or statements, to the child about his behavior which again does not communicate what they want the child to do. For example, the teacher discovers a child in the corner writing on the walls with crayons. Instead of demanding the child "Stop," the teacher may:

Make statement of fact: "Child, you are writing on the wall!" (NOTE: This statement is often followed by a question.)

Question the child: "Why are you doing that? What's wrong with you?"

Question the child as to whether he will stop the inappropriate behavior: "Will you please stop writing on the walls?" (NOTE: The teacher is not giving a clear demand with consequences for non-compliance.)

3. They may say all the right words—"stop fighting"— but not back up the words with the necessary consequences (loss of free time, suspension, etc.) to impress the child and influence the child to choose to eliminate the behavior. I worked with a 2nd grade teacher who illustrates this point well. She was quick to respond verbally with a firm request of what she wanted when a child behaved inappropriately. Her problem centered on two boys in her class whose disruptive behavior was not influenced by a mere "stop that," or "get to work." She was only able to assert her influence when she finally backed up her words with consequences ("get to work or you will not go to recess"). It took their missing several recesses before the boys realized they had an assertive teacher, one who was prepared to back up her words with actions, whenever needed.

4. They may demand the child stop, and threaten to follow through, but do not do so. This is a classic, non-assertive way of dealing with behavior problems. Look at this typical illustration

Sue gets out of her seat for the "umteenth" time that day.

Teacher: "Sue, I told you to stay in your seat; if you get out again you will lose your free time."

Sue gets out of her seat again.

Teacher: "Sue, I mean what I said. Get in your seat or you will lose your free time."

Sue gets out of her seat again.

Teacher: "Sue, are you deaf? I'm through talking with you. If I see you out of your seat one more time, and I mean one more time, there goes your free time!"

What often follows the non-assertive threat and no follow-through routine, is a final hostile outburst by the teacher.

Sue gets out of her seat again.

Teacher, storming over and grabbing her, yells: "You are the most disrespectful child I have ever worked with. You should be ashamed of yourself. I'm fed up with you and your attitude!"

5. They may plainly ignore the behavior, as if it never occurred. There was a 5th grade teacher whom a fellow professional worked with who would allow a child to wander around the room during work time. When my colleague asked her about this, she responded: "Oh, Jeff, he doesn't bother me. I let him do what he wants, he won't listen to me anyway, so why bother."

Non-assertive teachers also will respond in a "passive" manner when the children do as they please. Thus, the teachers do not utilize their potential impact to influence the child's appropriate behavior. More specifically, when a child does what they want, the teachers will, as mentioned before, *ignore* the child, or they:

1. Delay their response until much later when it will lose its impact. A kindergarten teacher we worked with would praise the children at the end of the day for their "good" behavior in the morning. This will have minimal influence on the behavior of children at that age.

2. Do not back their words up with the necessary actions. Some children may need more support than just a smile or a "well done" to influence their behavior. They may need additional support, be it a positive note to their parents, extra free time, or special time with the teacher, etc. If a teacher utilizes only verbal praise with such children, her responses will not have the desired influence on the child's behavior. A good example to illustrate this point would be a situation encountered by a colleague. The child, a 6th grader, was very hostile towards the teacher. When the teacher complimented the child on his behavior, he would quickly do the exact opposite. The teacher's verbal comments were not having the desired influence. What she had to do was back up her words with a consequence the child wanted. In this case she gave him a minute of free time (to be accumulated until the end of the day) whenever he behaved as she asked. The free time had the necessary impact to help him choose to increase his appropriate behavior.

Non-assertive teachers will often allow the children to manipulate them verbally. The children learn that they can get around the teacher if they just argue with them long enough.

Teacher: "Steve, I want you to clean up and get to work. It is work time."

Steve: "Just a few more minutes. You never allow me to finish my project."

Teacher: "All the other children are back to work."

Steve: "I know, but I just need a little more time."

Teacher: "You always want more time."

Steve: "Oh, just this last time, I won't ask you ever again."

Teacher: "You said that last time."

Steve: "I mean it, this time I promise!"

Teacher: "Oh alright, I'm tired of arguing with you. Do what you want, you won't listen to me anyway."

HOSTILE

A hostile teacher is one who responds in a manner which may get her needs met, but her response will disregard the needs and feelings of the children. She may violate the rights of the child in order to get her needs met. The hostile teacher will generally relate to the children in what could be described as a negative, condescending, or angry manner, which communicates to the child, "I don't like you" or "there is something wrong with you." Often the hostile teacher feels the only way to get a child to behave is to be mean and angry and express her wants by yelling and screaming. She will utilize discipline to "get back at the child," rather than help the child learn to behave more appropriately. The hostile teacher often views the classroom as a "battleground," with the children as the enemy.

More specifically, when it is necessary for a hostile teacher to respond to the inappropriate behavior of a child she may do one of the following:

1. **Use a "you" statement which conveys a negative "put down" message, but in no way clearly communicates to the child what the teacher wants.**

"You just don't understand because you never listen."

"You should be ashamed of how you behaved today."

"How many times do I have to talk to you?"

"You never act your age."

"You make me sick."

2. **Express their negative value judgments of the child and/or his behavior.**

"You are really stupid."

"That was a dumb thing you just did."

"You act like a little monster in this class."

"I have never had a child who was as lazy as you are."

"You have a disgusting attitude."

"Quit acting like such a baby."

Usually, both the "you" statements and negative value judgments are expressed in an angry tone of voice, or while the teacher is screaming or yelling at the child. In addition, these "put downs" are often expressed, to the embarrassment of the child, while his classmates are present.

3. Threaten the child in an angry manner with no evidence of consistent follow-through. When I was in school, I had a 4th grade teacher who would go around and angrily threaten us: "Stop that or you will be sorry," or "You just wait, I'll get you for this," or "If I see you do that again, you will be a very sorry little boy." She rarely followed through on her threats, but we were terrified by her constant angry outbursts.

4. Utilize follow-through consequences which are overly severe. The threatened consequences tend to be so unrealistic that the teacher will have difficulty enforcing them, or she will not want to enforce them when her anger subsides. I once observed a 3rd grade teacher who had a child that was very disruptive during P.E. One day she blew up at the child and told him that he would have to sit on the bench for the next *three* weeks during P.E. The next day she had him sit on the bench during P.E. But the following day a number of children were out sick, and they needed the boy to play so there would be enough players for a game. She allowed him to play that day, and forgot about the "benching" for the remainder of the three week period. Such over-reactions by hostile teachers are what we call "over-kill."

5. Physically respond to a child out of anger. This can include pulling a child up by the hair, squeezing the child's arm, throwing a child up against a wall, hitting a child. These are all responses designed to meet the teacher's need to release her anger, and *"hurt"* rather than help set limits for the child. Note the following extreme example from The Los Angeles Times (1975):

TEACHER'S CATTLE PROD NOT CRUEL, JUDGE RULES

Ottawa, Ill. (UPI)—A battery-powered cattle prod used by a teacher against unruly pupils is not "cruel" treatment, a judge has ruled.

A 10-page opinion handed down this week by LaSalle Circuit Judge Leonard Hoffman said the dictionary definition of "cruel" suggested something more severe than the jolt sixth-grade boys received from the prod used by teacher Frank J. Rolando III.

Rolando was fired in November, 1973, by the School Board in Oglesby on charges of cruel treatment.

Rolando had a serious disciplinary problem, the judge said. "Several of the boys would not remain in their seats, they made noises, shouted and screamed and at times stood on their desks. They threw paper wads, pencils, erasers and pens around the room and on occasions they displayed pornographic drawings to girls and used lewd and obscene language."

A hostile teacher will respond to the appropriate behavior of children with sarcastic responses. The teacher that comes to mind whenever we think of sarcasm is a 10th grade math teacher who had the "slow" learners. He didn't like "slow" learners and didn't hide the feeling very well. One day in his class, one of the students, Ralph, finally completed the assignment. It was the first time he had done so in two weeks. The teacher's response to Ralph was, "It's about time you did all the work. I can't believe you actually stopped playing around long enough to do it." We think that was the last assignment Ralph completed the entire year.

ASSERTIVE

An assertive teacher is one who clearly and firmly expresses her wants and feelings to the children and is prepared to back up her words with actions. She clearly tells the children what behavior is acceptable and which is unacceptable. The assertive teacher recognizes the fact that she has wants and needs and has the right to get them met in the classroom. She is also aware of her limitations and realizes that she has the right to ask for assistance in her efforts, be it from the principal, parent(s), or peers.

An assertive teacher has *positive expectations* of her ability to have influence on the behavior of her students. This positive attitude is reflected in her words and actions with the children. The assertive teacher is aware of the child's need for positive limits, and she is prepared to set those limits with both words and actions. At the same time, she is cognizant of the child's need for warmth and support and, thus, does not allow the child's appropriate behavior to go unrecognized. The assertive teacher, by her behavior, communicates to the children: "I care too much about you, to allow you to engage in inappropriate behavior, without my acting in a positive, limit-setting manner. I care too much about you, as well, to allow your appropriate behavior to go unnoticed by me. I also care too much about myself, to let you take advantage of my wants and feelings."

More specifically, an assertive teacher will *actively respond to a child's inappropriate behavior by clearly communicating to the child her disapproval of the behavior, followed by what she wants the child to do.*

"Stop talking with your neighbor, get to work!"

"I want you to stop shouting out, raise your hand!"

"You will stay in your seat during work time, now sit down!"

"I don't allow running in this classroom, now walk!"

An assertive teacher, in order to maximize her influence, is aware that her limit-setting response must be delivered in as effective a manner as is possible. This is well illustrated by a first grade teacher that we worked with. She had in her class a boy named Adam. Adam needed firm limits, especially during transitions between activities. He tended to get very excited and would from time to time begin to run around the classroom yelling and disrupting. When we were in the class, Adam was having a rough day, and he began to run around as the class was preparing to go to recess. His teacher walked up to him, put her hand on his shoulder, looked him in the eye and firmly said to him, "Adam, stop running, go sit on the mat!" Adam responded quickly to her request. How she told him what she wanted, the eye contact, the hand on his shoulder, etc., were just as important as what she said. All of these helped her communicate effectively what she wanted from him.

Whenever necessary the assertive teacher plans how to back up her limit-setting statements with appropriate consequences. This is done in order to maximize the influence her response can have on the behavior of the child. She realizes that she must be *prepared* to provide the child as meaningful a consequence as possible, to help influence the child to choose more appropriate behavior. If this means taking away an activity (free time, P.E.), sending the child to the principal, or calling the parents, etc., she will do so. The assertive teacher does not threaten to follow through on her demands: she promises to do so. If she tells a child that he will miss P.E. if he disrupts one more time, and the child chooses to disrupt, the child misses P.E.!

An assertive teacher is *persistent* in how she responds to the child's inappropriate behavior. A 6th grade teacher we worked with several years ago had a group of students who rarely finished their math. They would rather talk than work. The teacher gave them the choice of finishing their math during math time or they would have to do it during recess. He was prepared to miss his recesses to watch the students. It was necessary for him to keep most of the students in from their recess for a full week before they realized he meant what he said. Then they chose to get their work done when they were supposed to. Without the persistent follow-through the students probably never would have chosen to finish their math.

In response to a *child's appropriate behavior*, an *assertive teacher* is *quick both to recognize it and express this recognition to the child.* This may be done verbally: "Good work," "I like the way you cleaned up," "That's a real improvement over last week's behavior," "Keep up the good work," and non-verbally: smile, pat on the shoulder, wink, etc.

Whenever required, she is prepared to back up her words with consequences in order to motivate the behavior of more difficult children. She is aware some children need more support and attention than others and she is prepared to provide the children with as much of both as she reasonably can. An excellent teacher we worked with really knew how to back up her words with the necessary consequences. In her 2nd grade class she had a boy with numerous personal problems who was in need of all the positive attention he could get. In order to give him the support for his appropriate behavior that he needed, she not only praised him whenever she could, but she also allowed him to earn time with her as a consequence for his appropriate behavior. They would spend the time alone together reading his favorite stories. The time with her was something he desperately needed, and this provided the motivation he needed to help him maintain his appropriate behavior in the classroom.

An assertive teacher will be persistent in the verbal responses she makes to the children. She will say what she means and mean what she says. Referring back to the example of Steve and his situation of cleaning up and getting to work, an assertive teacher may sound as follows:

Teacher: "Steve, I want you to clean up and get to work."

Steve: "Just a few more minutes. You never allow me to finish my project."

Teacher (looking Steve in the eye): "I said I want you to clean up and get to work."

Steve: "I know but just a little more time please?"

Teacher: "Steve, no more time. I want you to get to work now!"

Plainly stated, an assertive teacher is prepared to function in an active "take charge" manner in the classroom. She is the leader of the classroom, and utilizes planning, persistence and positive expectations to help meet her needs and those of the students.

THE EFFECTS OF THE NON-ASSERTIVE, ASSERTIVE, AND HOSTILE RESPONSE STYLES

Just as you, as the teacher, must learn to discriminate the difference between response styles in your daily interaction, it is important to have an understanding of the effects that each response style will characteristically have on the teacher-child relationship. No one incident, and the way you handle it, will guarantee the following effects because, as we said earlier, no one is "always" assertive, aggressive, or non-assertive. What we can say is that when your characteristic responses tend to fall in any of the general response styles, you can expect any or all of the following general results.

Non-Assertive

The non-assertive teacher pays a price and exacts a cost from her students as a result of her passive "wishy-washy" behavior. Such a response style results in a classroom environment in which there is a constant testing of wills between the "powerless" teacher and the students. Both teacher and students will feel either frustrated, inadequate, or manipulated.

A non-assertive teacher will feel frustrated and inadequate due to her inability to get her needs met in the classroom. The stress she experiences will eventually result in her becoming "burned out" and fed up with children and her profession. You will hear her say things like, "I give up with those kids, they don't want to learn anyway. I'm fed up with the hassles and headaches they give me." The frustration she feels will often stay with her when she leaves school and will have a negative impact on her personal as well as professional life.

The non-assertive teacher feels a good deal of inner hostility towards the children she feels she "cannot" handle. This hostility may not be openly expressed to the children, or it may suddenly burst forth in a hostile response by the teacher. This hostility is a serious block to the development of a positive teacher-child relationship.

The students of a non-assertive teacher feel frustrated, manipulated, and angry. They do not experience the clear limits they need to function in the classroom. One day the teacher may mean what she says, the next three she doesn't. The children may have to sit through barrages of threats which they have little way of knowing if they are real or meaningless. The children will resent this situation, and many will try to get away with all they can. They will "test" the teacher continuously to see if she does or doesn't mean what she says that day. The children will learn to "con" the teacher in order to manipulate her around what limits are set. The lack of limits and the inevitable testing by the children result in a chaotic environment of constant disruption, which damages the children educationally and emotionally.

The children will also learn that their appropriate behavior goes basically unnoticed, thus there is little motivation from the teacher to behave appropriately. You may hear the students say: "It is easier, and more fun to just goof off in her class. She won't really do anything to you even if she does catch you. In our class even some of the 'good' children act up just for the fun of it." In general, the children will feel little or no respect for a non-assertive teacher and thus behave accordingly towards her.

Hostile

The hostile teacher, as well, exacts a dear cost for her behavior from both the children and herself. The negative emphasis of a hostile response style tends to create a negative environment and affects the way teacher and child feel about themselves and each other.

Contrary to the belief of most students, no teacher likes to be "mean" and hostile. The teacher exercises a negative stance because she feels it is the only way she can maintain control. Most teachers are afraid to let go of their "iron grip" for they feel it is the only way they can get the children to do what they want. They don't like being the way they are; and thus, most feel guilty about how they deal with the children. The fear, guilt, and negative responses become a major stumbling block to the development of anything but a negative, self-defeating teacher-child relationship.

Children quickly learn to fear and dislike hostile teachers. The teacher often becomes the "enemy." The children do what they can, be it lie, cheat, feign illness, to get around the perceived unfair negative limits of the teacher. In such a hostile environment such inappropriate behavior may become acceptable to the children in order that they don't have to face the wrath of the teacher. You will hear children say, "That teacher is so mean, I'll do anything not to get her after me. I don't like the way I behave, but I'm afraid if she finds out I made a mistake or had an accident she'll 'murder' me."

The often unexpressed hostility the children feel towards the teacher can at times end up being displaced
upon their peers. After a morning of being berated and
belittled, the children not only feel "put down" but also
angry. During recess it would not be unusual to witness
a good deal of teasing, poking, and fighting between the
children as they attempt to release the frustrations built
up from the morning in the classroom.

Many children do what is asked of them in a hostile
teacher's classroom. They behave out of anxiety and/or
fear. They learn not only to dislike the teacher, but school
as well. The negative atmosphere also wears away at the
self-image and self-concept of the children. After a negative day at school a child who feels O.K. about himself
will feel a little less O.K. A child who does not feel O.K.
will feel even worse. These feelings come home with the
child and often can result in the parents having more difficulty with discipline and/or difficulty in getting the
child to go to school, period.

Assertive

The assertive teacher creates an environment in which
both she and the child have an opportunity to get their
needs met. The atmosphere is basically positive with a
balance established between the rights of the children
and the teacher, and between firm limits and warmth
and support.

The assertive teacher, through her behavior, takes the
responsibility to get her needs met in the classroom. By
getting her needs fulfilled, she is more capable of thus
meeting the needs of the children, and thus reaping the
internal and external benefits one gets from performing

well professionally. This does not mean that an assertive teacher's behavior results in a "perfect" classroom, where all is "sweetness and light," where all the children learn and behave to their full potential, or where she never has a rough day with the children. What it does mean is that the assertive teacher has the satisfaction of knowing she has accepted her professional responsibility and has done everything in her "power" to do the best job she was capable of doing.

The children learn to trust and respect an assertive teacher. They know that the teacher means what she says, and says what she means. The children clearly know the parameters of acceptable and unacceptable behavior. Thus they have the opportunity to choose how they want to behave while knowing fully what the consequences will be for their behavior. As one child put it: "He is a fair teacher. If you're good he'll let you know he likes it, and if you're bad, 'Man,' he will 'get on your case' until you stop. You know he's there with you all the time. It really feels 'kinda neat,' I dig the guy!"

If you note, we didn't state the children will all like the assertive teacher, or all the children will behave. Some children may not like the teacher for any number of reasons. Some children may still choose not to behave, for any number of reasons. All that an assertive teacher can do by her behavior is try to establish an atmosphere where she maximizes the *potential* for a positive teacher-child relationship developing between her and each and every child.

Sample Situations

In order to give you practice in discriminating between non-assertive, assertive, and hostile response styles, here are examples of typical situations confronted by teachers. For each situation we will provide you a typical nonassertive, hostile, and assertive response. These in no way exhaust the possible responses to each situation nor is the assertive response given the *only way* to respond "correctly." It is only one way of responding assertively.

A 3rd grade teacher had a number of children who frequently would push and shove in order to be first in line. This would result in constant fighting and yelling before the class went outside. Before lunch the problem occurs again.

Non-Assertive Response
The teacher walks up to the children and states, "I don't know what's wrong with you children. You're pushing and shoving again. You children need to learn how to line up like good boys and girls. Now I want you all to try to do so."

Hostile Response
The teacher walks up to the children who were pushing and grabs them and roughly yanks them to the back of the line. Once they are at the end of the line she angrily states, "You push and shove others, I'll push and shove you!"

Assertive Response
The teacher firmly tells the children, "Stop pushing and shoving." To back up her words, she makes all the children who were pushing and shoving go to the back of the line.

A 6th grade boy habitually stole supplies from the classroom and would then lie when confronted about his stealing. The boy was very clever and the teacher had never had actual proof of the child's stealing. One day the teacher found the boy outside of class with some stolen supplies.

Non-Assertive Response
   The teacher takes the supplies back stating, "You should know better than this. Stealing is wrong and you should never do this. I don't ever want to *catch* you stealing again. If I *catch* you, you'll be sorry."

Hostile Response
   The teacher yells at the child, "You're just a little thief. I knew you were stealing and now I have caught you and you're going to get it. When I'm done with you, you'll be sorry you ever stepped foot in my class."

Assertive Response
   The teacher tells the child, "I will not tolerate any child stealing from my classroom. We are going to go right to the principal's office and I'm going to call your parents to discuss your stealing with them."

In a 2nd grade classroom there was a child who was quite immature for his age and had a good deal of difficulty playing and sharing with his peers. One morning his teacher observed him sharing his blocks and playing in a positive manner with two other children.

Non-Assertive Response
   The teacher thinks to herself, "That's the first he has played so well with the other children. That's real progress for him." She does not, though, communicate her recognition or support to the child.

Hostile Response
   The teacher walks up to the boy and states, "Finally

you're acting your age, and not carrying on like a kinder-
gartener.''

Assertive Response
    The teacher goes up to him, puts her arm around him
and states, ''I really like seeing you share and play so well
with the other children.''

A kindergarten teacher had a girl who would get disruptive during the transition periods between activities.
The girl would get very excited, fail to follow directions,
and frequently ran around the room yelling. The teacher
began setting firm limits, and one afternoon the girl
cleaned up appropriately and came directly to the rug
as instructed.

Non-Assertive Response
    The teacher simply does not verbally or non-verbally
recognize or support the girl's appropriate behavior.

Hostile Response
    The teacher states to the girl, ''It's about time I didn't
have to chase you around the room to get you to clean up
and sit down!''

Assertive Response
    The teacher says to the girl, ''I liked the excellent job
you did cleaning up and following directions. You did so
well you may sit on my lap and pick the story that I will
now read to the class.''

An 8th grade science teacher had a problem with students frequently cheating on tests. During an exam he
observed several students openly looking at each others'
papers.

Non-Assertive Response
The teacher states, "Don't forget, I have told you if I catch anyone cheating they will be sorry. So I hope any of you who may be thinking of cheating won't do it."

Hostile Response
He storms up to the students and rips up their papers angrily stating, "I hate cheaters. You should be ashamed of yourselves."

Assertive Response
He calls the students to his desk and firmly states, "There is no cheating in this class! I saw you looking at each other's papers, so you all get an 'F' on the test."

In a 6th grade class there was a very belligerent child who would constantly confront the teacher's authority by refusing to do his work. The teacher had repeatedly demanded he do his work to no avail. One afternoon the teacher told the class to work on their math. Instead of getting to work the boy began to doodle on his math worksheet. The teacher walks up to him and asks him to get to work. The child angrily responds, "I don't give a darn what you say, I don't want to do your dumb work."

Non-Assertive Response
The teacher states, "You never talk to me like that again. Get to work." The child just sits there and does nothing. The teacher does not back her words up with an appropriate limit setting follow-through consequence.

Hostile Response
The teacher angrily grabs the child and shouts, "Keep your big filthy mouth shut. If you open your mouth again I'll slap it shut."

Assertive Response
   The teacher firmly states, "You never talk back to me again! Now you have a choice, get to work immediately or I will suspend you this instant!"

   A 9th grade Social Studies teacher had a boy who was the classic "class clown." He would frequently make irrelevant comments during discussions or act "silly" coming and going from class. Whenever he acted appropriately and the teacher praised him in front of his peers, he would get embarrassed and act up even more disruptively. One class period he was serious and participated very well during the class discussion.

Non-Assertive Response
   The teacher stated in front of his classmates, "Mark, I really like the way you participated." Mark immediately stood up and took a bow in front of his peers. He continued to "clown" until the bell rang.

Hostile Response
   The teacher stated, "It's nice to see you don't have to act like a fool all of the time."

Assertive Response
   The teacher took Mark aside after class and told him, "I was very pleased with how well you contributed during class today."

ROADBLOCKS TO
ASSERTIVE DISCIPLINE

We all have within us the assertive potential to get the majority of our needs met in the classroom. The major problem most of us encounter is our personal "roadblocks" which hinder our becoming more assertive. The most common "roadblock" for the majority of teachers is their *negative expectation* of their ability to deal effectively with the behavior of their students. This is especially true in relation to students with special needs and/or problems. This relates back to the point made before: Teachers are trained to deal only with "normal" students. As a direct result, most teachers, when confronted with "problem" students, lose track of their assertive potential and feel that basically they can't get the student to behave in an appropriate manner. This point is well illustrated in the following vignette.

Philip came to his new elementary school after having been expelled from a neighboring school, because of his "uncontrollable" behavior. His behavior had been so "bad" that at one time he had been in therapy with a local child psychologist for over a year.

The first few days Philip responded well to his new environment; and his teacher, Ms. J., was optimistic of her ability to work successfully with him in her classroom. As the weeks progressed and Philip began to exhibit his "uncontrollable" behavior (i.e., running around the room, hitting other children, not attending to academic tasks), Ms. J. began to feel more and more frustrated and inadequate in her ability to get him to change his behavior. It seemed that although her usual methods of discipline with Philip had an immediate effect, the effects were short-lived.

As her feeling of inadequacy and frustration grew, she began to wonder, "Why won't he listen to me? There has to be something 'wrong with that boy.' " Consulting with the principal, she was informed of Philip's past psychiatric history. It became clear to her that Philip was "emotionally disturbed," and because of his problems he was unable to control his behavior. Therefore, it was impossible for him to respond to the limits placed on the other children in the school.

Since she did not expect him to change, her methods of control became more and more ineffective. Her general response was to remove him from any situation that "he could not handle" (i.e., when he hurt a child while standing in line, she excused him from standing in line again). In essence, she attempted to protect herself from any situation which would require her to be assertive with him.

Philip is what we call a "powerful child": A child that the teacher feels has problems (real or imagined) which prevent him from being able to behave appropriately. As a result, the teacher feels she is incapable of influencing the child to behave in an appropriate manner. Some of the most common problems that teachers feel prevent them from being able to deal effectively with a child can be divided into eight general areas.

Emotional Illness. The child is "sick" and thus cannot be expected to act "normal." Without "treatment" the child will not be "cured" and be able to behave appropriately (i.e., "he is seeing a psychiatrist; he is really a 'disturbed' child. Until he works out his 'hangups' there is nothing I can do with him in class.").

Heredity. The child was born with a genetic make-up

that compels him to act in an inappropriate manner. The child's condition can originate from: parental characteristics ("His father did poorly in school also. I guess it just runs in the family."); his racial or genetic heritage ("Black children just all seem to fight a lot; that's just the way they are. We can't really do anything about it."); or, a specific defect ("The parents say he was born 'nasty,' and, as the teacher, I agree that there is no way to get to that child.").

Brain Damage (M.B.D. and Hyperactivity). The child, because of brain damage, cannot be expected to follow directions, keep from disrupting, or stay in his seat. It is physically impossible for the child to comply in class (i.e., "He cannot help it, the doctor thinks he's hyperactive and you know what that means—he has to have Ritalin or I can't work with him at all.").

Ignorance. The child is not mature enough to behave in an appropriate manner; he doesn't understand what he is doing (i.e., "You just can't get him to understand there are rules in this classroom.").

Peer Pressure. The child is easily influenced by his peers, such that he is unable to control himself when he is around them (i.e., "He is fine until he gets with those other boys and girls, then there is no way to get him to behave.").

Inadequate Parenting. The parents have not provided the child the love, the attention, the discipline, or the security necessary for him to be able to behave appropriately (i.e., "What can you expect from the child coming from parents like those?").

Socio-Economic Background. The child is from such a deprived socio-economic background (i.e., "poverty") that he can't be expected to behave as other children do (i.e., "Living in his neighborhood, of course he gets into trouble all the time. What else would you expect from him?").

Classroom Environment. The child cannot function in a regular classroom, an open structure classroom, etc.: The child needs to be in a special class (i.e., Educationally Handicapped), or a special school (i.e., "That child just can't be expected to function in a regular classroom. If only we had an E.H. class for him to be in.").

All of these are *real problems* that can affect the behavior of children and make it more difficult for them to behave appropriately. But, these problems do not prevent the teacher from being able to influence the child's behavior, given the proper methods. Children with these problems *can* behave, when they want to do so: They *choose* not to behave. In other words, they won't behave.

We need to discuss the "can't behave vs. won't behave" issue in more detail. "Can't behave" connotes a child out of control, a child whose behavior cannot be influenced by you. Very few children cannot control their own behavior, and they usually have organic or physical problems. Here are some examples of what we mean:

A teacher had a child in her class with cerebral palsy. His physical problems affected his large muscle coordination. Even though the child tried, because of his physical problems he was unable to keep up with the class whenever they walked across the school grounds or went on a field trip. The child's inability to keep pace with the other children could cause problems at times. There was, however, no way the teacher could influence the boy to walk faster. Assertive demands of "walk faster!" and/or praise or support would have had no positive effect because of the extent of the child's physical handicap.

Another teacher had in her class a child with epilepsy. He would periodically have grand mal seizures, which of course frightened the other children and totally disrupted the class. Again, there was no way the teacher could influence the child to stop having his seizures. Could you imagine how ludicrous it would be for the teacher to stand over the child and demand he "stop having a seizure!" It sounds so ludicrous because the child could not physically control his behavior.

Now, compare the children in the previous examples, who truly can't control their behavior, to the typical child with behavior problems, say, for example, a Philip. Philip *can* control his behavior. Philip did control his behavior the first few days of school. Children like Philip *choose* when they want to and don't want to behave appropriately. Again, they *won't* behave.

The classic example of this point can be illustrated by the following. In our school consultations each year, we are called upon to observe hundreds of children with classroom behavior problems. When we observe the children for the first time, we rarely, and we mean rarely, observe any children who engage in inappropriate behavior. Why is this so? Are we so assertive that our mere presence in a classroom gets the children to "shape up?" We wish it were so! What occurs is as follows. The children we are observing, be it because of intuition, the teacher's telling them, our actions, or their paranoia, usually realize we are there to observe them. The children, not knowing us, do not know how we will respond to them, especially if they are disruptive. For all they know, these observers will take them out of class, report them to their parents, and/or much worse. Thus, the children, out of fear of the unknown consequences, usually choose to behave appropriately for the initial period of time that we observe them. The children clearly demonstrate to us and their teachers that they *can* behave appropriately when they want to and, thus, *won't* behave when they *don't* want to. There is much more than semantics involved in the "can't vs won't" issue. If you feel the child can't behave, or you can't influence him to behave, there is little or nothing you can, or will, do to change his behavior. So, then, why bother to be assertive? If you feel the child won't behave, then you need to determine a method to influence his behavior assertively in order that he chooses to behave appropriately. You thus have the responsibility to utilize your potential influence with such a child. What you will need to do is to determine how to assert yourself to maximize the influence you can have on the child.

What this all comes down to, again, is your *expectations* of your ability to influence the child's behavior. To illustrate the point further, let's go back to the example of Ms. J. and Philip.

Philip naturally responded to the lowered expectations placed upon him and began to act more and more "disturbed." The situation reached a crisis when he attempted to stab a classmate with his pencil. His parents were brought in, and they proved to be of no help because of the tremendous hostility they felt toward their child.

As a last resort, Ms. J. sought consultation from the school mental health consultant. As she went over Philip's case with the consultant, it became clear to her that she was not only frustrated and overwhelmed in her attempts to help Philip, but as each attempt failed, she would come up with reasons why his behavior couldn't be changed, and why she was so non-assertive.

The consultant pointed out several key reasons that Ms. J. believed were the cause of her problems with Philip: 1) Philip was "emotionally disturbed" and therefore could not be expected to act normal.
2) His parents did not provide him with a secure, loving home with firm limits, and therefore it was impossible for Philip to develop a sense of trust towards the adults in school.
3) Because of his "uncontrollable" behavior, it became clear that Philip could not function in the openness of the school environment and needed a much smaller classroom setting.

At this point the following dialog took place between the consultant and Ms. J.

Ms. J.: "Well, you have done a good job of summing up Philip's problems, but that doesn't help me any. I still don't know what to do to get him to behave."

Consultant: "At what time does he behave?"

Teacher: "When he wants to!"

Consultant: "Like, when, for example?"

Teacher: "Oh, say, if we are having a field trip and he knows he has to be good to go. He will be good for a day or so before. But I don't have field trips every other day to motivate him to behave."

Consultant: "So he *can* at times behave when he wants to."

Teacher: "Yes, but it is all too rare."

Consultant: "Have you ever been able to get him to stop any problem behavior?"

Teacher: "I can't think of any instance. Oh, wait a minute. Philip once tried to get into my purse. I told him to put my purse down, never touch it again, and if he did I would have him suspended on the spot!"

Consultant: "You were sure assertive with him. I bet he has never touched your purse again."

Teacher: "You're right, but how did you know he has never come near my purse since?"

Consultant: "Because you were so assertive. You obviously said what you wanted and were prepared to back up your words with actions."

Teacher: "You're right, I was. But, I don't want to have to threaten him with suspension to get him to behave."

Consultant: "Are you aware of what you have been saying?"

Teacher: "No, I don't follow you."

Consultant: "You just said he *could* behave if you really became assertive with him. What about his emotional problems, etc., that prevented him from being able to behave?"

Teacher: "What you just said is true. He does behave when I really crack down on him. He *can* behave. Darn it, he just does not want to! He just tries to run me. And you know what, I was making excuses for him, and myself. I was blaming it all on his parents, his emotional problems, and all that."

Consultant: "That's correct, he can behave, when you

are assertive. You can influence his behavior. It may require you to utilize skills and methods you don't usually need with the other children, but you can do it."

Teacher: "O.K., I see what you mean. He can behave, but what is it going to take for me to get him to do so all of the time?"

Consultant: "You have taken the first step. You have changed your expectations, and you can now see that you really do have an influence over his behavior."

We have illustrated how your negative expectations can be a crucial "roadblock." Now here are the methods that we, and the teachers we have worked with, have found effective to raise their expectations and overcome this "roadblock" to dealing assertively with students.

Deal Realistically with the Child and Your Potential Influence on His Behavior. You can influence the behavior of your students no matter what problems they may have! (The only qualification to this statement would be organic problems, such as epilepsy, etc.) What you want to accept is that for many "powerful children" your usual methods of discipline simply will not work! If you want to get your needs and the students' needs met, you will have to utilize different methods of dealing with their behavior. With some students you may have to be "firmer" in dealing with their disruptive behavior; with others you may need to be more "positive" in dealing with their appropriate behavior. Here is a typical example of what we are saying.

Ms. M. taught 2nd grade. When students in her class disrupted, she had them sit in the corner until they calmed down. This approach worked with all of the students, except for a very high strung, volatile boy named Mark. When he was sent to the corner, he would scream and upset the entire class. Ms. M. felt overwhelmed by his behavior and believed Mark was just too "wild" for her to handle. She discussed her problems with a fellow teacher who had been Mark's teacher the year before. Her peer pointed out that in order for her to get Mark to stop his emotional outbursts, she would consistently have to call his parents after each outburst, and have them follow through at home. His parents were cooperative, and Mark would "shape up" quickly when his parents dealt with him. Ms. M. had never found it necessary to follow through so firmly and consistently with a child in her entire career, but obviously something had to be done. She thus began calling Mark's parents whenever he became disruptive, and they would follow through at home. Within two weeks, Mark chose to stop his outbursts and behave in class like the other children.

Accept the Reality that You Have the Right to Set Firm Limits, And that All Students Need them. A number of teachers feel ineffective because they are reluctant to set firm limits upon the disruptive behavior of their students. This can be for any number of reasons. Some teachers may feel that if they are "too strict" the students will not like them and/or turn-off to education. The simplest response to that statement is the following question. Which teachers do you have the most positive memories of? We guarantee you they were teachers who set firm, positive limits in their classrooms and let you know they were in charge of the class.

Other teachers feel "sorry" for children who have problems, and feel that to set firm limits and follow through on those limits with these children would further harm already troubled children. Unfortunately, it is reality that all too many children have to deal with problems resulting from negligent parents, inadequate home life, poverty, racism, etc. Many of these problems can prove to be emotionally or educationally crippling. Our position, based upon our work with students, is this: If you allow such children to go undisciplined, or allow them to act in an inappropriate manner without firmly responding, in the long run you will do them incredibly more harm than if you set firm limits with them. *Problems or no problems, no child should be allowed to engage in behavior that is self-destructive or violates the rights of his peers or teacher.* The following vignette illustrates this point.

Mary was a 1st grader with many severe emotional problems. In class, Mary would constantly provoke the other children, both verbally and physically. Her teacher, Ms. C., aware of Mary's problems, felt protective of her and attempted to counsel Mary whenever her frequent provocations towards the other children got out of hand. By mid-year, Mary's behavior had become such a constant problem that there was a constant air of tension between her and her classmates, and her teacher. Ms. C. tried to reinforce Mary's behavior positively when Mary acted appropriately, but it did not help. Ms. C. was at her wits' end when she finally began to realize the result of her overprotectiveness: (1) Mary was having to deal with the stress of constant conflicts with her peers; (2) the other students were having their rights violated by the constant provocations; and (3) her own personal needs were not being met because of the constant disruptions resulting from Mary's behavior. Ms. C. then sat down with Mary and assertively let her know that she would not tolerate any further provocations by her. Ms. C. decided that whenever Mary did provoke another child she would have to sit in the corner until she calmed down. Some days she had to go to the corner 4 or 5 times. However, Mary quickly tired of this and began to control her behavior. As a direct result, her relationships with her peers, and with the teacher, improved markedly. Mary still had problems in other areas, but now her school experience was a more positive and productive one for her.

Accept the Reality that You Have the Right to Ask for Assistance in Limit Setting from the Principal, Peers, etc. Some teachers are simply afraid to set firm limits upon the disruptive behavior of certain children. This is especially true when teachers deal with children who are extremely emotional, or who exhibit violent or bizarre behavior. Teachers dealing with such students fear that if they confront the child, the child may become "out of control," and/or respond in a manner the teacher cannot, or does not, want to handle. Thus, the teachers basically attempt, whenever possible, to stay clear of any confrontations with such students. The net result of this situation is that the teachers end up intimidated by such students, to the detriment of all.

Whenever you are afraid or intimidated by such students, it is obvious that you will need additional assistance in dealing effectively with them. When such students get agitated and/or severely disrupt your class, you will need to be prepared to receive help from other adults, principal, aide, counselor, etc., with your limit-setting efforts. Note the following example.

Ms. H. was a 7th grade teacher. In her class she had an extremely hostile boy with a violent temper. Often when he was asked to do his work he would angrily refuse, and if pushed he would start to have a tantrum (on several occasions he had thrown objects at the teacher). When Ms. H. demanded he leave the room, he would refuse, and because of his size and strength, she could not get him out. The frustrations and anxiety created by several of those outbursts caused Ms. H. to stay clear of any limit-setting confrontations with the child. Eventually, though, his behavior became more and more disruptive, and something had to be done. Realizing that she could not, on her own, deal with his behavior, she elicited the support of her vice-principal. Whenever the boy began to disrupt, she would buzz the vice-principal and he would come to her room and firmly escort the boy from her room. The vice-principal had to do this on three separate occasions. After that, the boy realized he could no longer get away with his acting up, and chose to do his work without any further incident.

Ask for Assistance from the Student's Parents. Many teachers could significantly increase their effectiveness if they appropriately utilized the assistance of the student's parents in their discipline efforts. This topic is discussed at length in the chapter "Asking for Help."

Accept the Reality that Certain Students Require Additional Positive Motivators to Influence Them to Behave Appropriately. Just as some students require firmer limits than others, some students require additional motivators in order to influence their appropriate behavior. For some students, praise, or high grades alone, will not motivate them to increase their positive behavior. With such students you will need to determine motivators that will prove influential with them. Unless you recognize this reality and deal with it, you will severely limit your effectiveness with certain students.

Ms. K. was a veteran 4th grade teacher. In all of her years of teaching she had never felt, nor had, the need to motivate her students with more than a little praise or an occasional pat on the back. The year we worked with her, though, she had a student named Raymond, an immature child in need of a great deal of attention from adults. He was a constant problem in class, continuously engaging in behavior designed to get Ms. K.'s attention (i.e., shouting out, coming up to her desk, etc.). She had been firm with him, but he continued his attention-getting disruptions. When we met with Ms. K. we pointed out that Raymond's behavior indicated that he needed more positive attention from her than the other students. We concluded by telling her that she would never have her needs met unless she provided him with positive attention. At first Ms. K. wanted no part of what we were saying and responded, "I treat all the children the same. He is just going to have to be good, period!"

Raymond's behavior became even more disruptive, and Ms. K. met with us again. This time she stated, "I don't know what to do with that kid, he's not like the other children. He can't ever seem to get enough attention from me. It seems as though he likes it when I yell and scream at him." We agreed with her that he needed more attention and arranged for him to get it in a more positive manner. Ms. K. decided to allow Raymond to earn time alone with her after school, depending upon his appropriate behavior. For every half-hour that he went without disrupting her, he would earn 1 minute of time with her. He could earn 10 minutes total each day. After school he would help her straighten up the room or simply sit and talk with her. Raymond immediately responded to the extra positive attention he was earning with her and quickly chose to eliminate his disruptions in class. Ms. K. summed up the situation well when she stated, "I can't believe how his behavior has improved. That boy was going to get my attention one way or the other. It sure makes my day, and his day, easier to give him those few minutes each day after school."

Utilize Assertive Skills. For you to reach your assertive potential, you need to have more than confidence in your ability, you also need to have specific discipline skills. In the following chapters we will present to you basic *Assertive Discipline* skills. These will enable you to increase your effectiveness in dealing with the behavior of your students, whether or not they possess any special problems or needs.

YOUR WANTS
AND NEEDS:

WHAT ARE THEY?
HOW DO YOU
GET THEM MET?

What are your needs in the classroom? What do you want the students to do? Simple question? Not for most teachers, and here is why. In recent years we in education have put heavy emphasis upon the needs of the students. As a result, most teachers have not recognized the importance of carefully determining *their own specific needs* in the classroom.

When we ask teachers what they want from their students, we typically hear responses such as:

"I want the kids to act good."

"I'm not sure what I specifically want, but I guess I want them to be good citizens and have a positive attitude."

"I want the children to respect me and each other."

"I don't want hassles from the boys who are trouble-makers."

These responses are vague and subjective. What is meant by "act good"? What are "good citizens"? How would you know if the students were demonstrating "respect"? What is meant by "hassles"?

If you are going to become more assertive, you have to analyze carefully the *specific behaviors* you want and need from your students. By specific behaviors we mean "sit in seat" or "follow directions," rather than "act good"; or, "share supplies," "take turns," "keep hands to self," rather than be "good citizens"; or, finally, "no fighting, lying, or shouting out," rather than simply no "hassles."

To assist you, here are examples of specific behaviors teachers typically want and need from their students:

follow directions
keep hands, feet, and
  objects to self
raise hand before speaking
no cussing or swearing
clean up
low noise level
walk in the classroom
complete work on time
no fighting
work independently
no back talk
no stealing
tell the truth
no destroying property

line up
come to class on time
no eating in class
use all supplies
  appropriately
listen to who is speaking
speak one at a time
play cooperatively on the yard
share supplies
take turns at activities
no screaming
work independently
stay in the classroom
keep legs of the chair
  on the floor

It is vital that you determine the behaviors that are needed from your students for you to function to your maximum potential in your classroom. We have found it useful to limit the number of behaviors that are determined to a maximum of five. These five behaviors can serve as the general rules for your class. Some teachers we work with humorously describe the five behaviors as those they need to "maintain their sanity in their classroom." An example of the five behaviors teachers may typically determine they need from their students would include:

1. Follow directions

2. Complete all assignments

3. Do not leave the classroom without permission

4. Work independently

5. Keep hands, feet, and objects to oneself

Word of warning: Do any of your wants and needs violate the best interest of your students? Do you want behavior from students that is unrealistic to expect, such as wanting kindergarten students to sit quietly for long periods of time? Do you want and need behavior that is not your right to ask, such as needing your students to come to you and share their personal problems? Again, the goal of *Assertive Discipline* is to maximize your potential in meeting your own needs, while in no way infringing upon or violating the rights of the students.

Once you have determined the behaviors you want, you will need to communicate them clearly to your students. You may choose to do this verbally and/or nonverbally. When verbally telling your students what you want, be clear and concise in your message. For example:

"As your teacher there are behaviors I need from you (my students) to do the best possible job. I expect the following from you: follow my directions, complete all assignments on time, work independently, there will be no fighting, and listen to me. It is my responsibility to let you know both when you are and when you are not doing what I want and need, and I will do so."

You also may want to make a sign which lists your wants and post it in your class. Some teachers have their students write down the behaviors and keep them in their desks. Other teachers "ditto" the behaviors they want and give them out to their students.

Let's now expand upon your basic wants and needs. Throughout a typical school day your wants and needs will change, depending upon the activity you wish the students to engage in. *No matter what the activity, in order to be assertive, you need to be aware of what behaviors you want and need from the students.* Most of these behaviors may be encompassed in the five behaviors you have already identified, although some may not.

In order to identify effectively and fulfill your wants and needs, it would be useful to categorize the various "activity periods" you utilize during your day. A typical elementary-level classroom would have any or all of the following general activity periods during a week: quiet work, rug time, discussion time, transition periods, independent work, free choice, P.E., art, music, and library. For each activity period, you should determine several specific wants and needs which are important to you.

Quiet Work
1. No talking
2. Follow directions
3. Complete assignments

Rug Time
1. Sit on rug
2. Keep hands to self
3. Raise hands

Transition Periods
1. Follow directions
2. Walk
3. Clean up

Free Choice
1. Choose an activity
2. Follow directions
3. Share supplies

P.E.
1. Follow directions
2. Take turns
3. Use equipment appropriately

Once you have identified your needs for each of your class's activity periods, you will need to communicate them to the students. A useful method we have found is as follows. Make a separate sign for each activity period with its name on it (i.e., QUIET WORK). Before you begin each new activity period, hold up the sign and explain to the students what you want (i.e., "This is the QUIET WORK sign. Whenever it is posted, there will be no talking, and you are to do your own work!"). You may need to utilize 5 to 9 signs during a typical school week. Each time you change activities you will need to post the appropriate sign. Most teachers assign a student monitor to do this. When used properly, the signs will serve two functions: (1) they will remind the students of the behavior you want during that activity, and (2) they will remind you of the behavior you need to respond assertively to.

One last word on determining your needs. For many teachers the most difficult days are those that include special activities such as field trips, assemblies, culminations, etc. One key reason they are so difficult is that the teachers do not determine their specific needs for such activities, and thus the students do not clearly know what is expected of them. Before a special activity is to take place, determine your needs and communicate them to your students.

Now that you have an idea of how to determine what you want and need in your classroom, it is time to look at how you are, or are not, getting these needs met.

There are few activities that are more difficult than taking a cold, hard look at one's own behavior. On the other hand, there are few activities that can be more useful. When you are attempting to develop more assertive responses, it is necessary to know how you typically respond to your students' behaviors. When the students do what you want, how do you generally respond—assertively, non-assertively, or hostilely? When the children do something you don't want them to do, how do you generally respond—assertively, non-assertively, or hostilely? Are the responses that you feel are "assertive" influencing the children's behavior in the way you want? Are your hostile responses setting necessary limits—or, are they succeeding only in putting down the child?

We have developed the following criteria to assist you in accurately analyzing both your strengths and weaknesses in relation to your ability to get your needs met.

1. How effectively do you communicate your wants and needs to your students? Do you clearly and specifically let your students know what behaviors you do or do not want them to engage in? Or do you tell them to "be good," "act nice," etc.? If we came into your classroom would your students be able to tell us specifically what you want them to be doing at that moment? Could you tell us?

2. How effectively do you verbally assert yourself? We divide this skill area into two distinct aspects: (a) how effectively do you verbally respond when the children do not do what you want *(Verbal Limit Setting)*; and, (b) how effectively do you verbally respond when the children do what you want *(Positive Verbal Assertions)*? We make a distinction for this reason: You may be consistently assertive when it comes to responding verbally to disruptive behavior, but tend to ignore or be weak in your verbal responses to appropriate or positive behavior. Or, you may respond in just the opposite manner. You may have trouble responding assertively when the children are "acting up," but are consistently praising them when they are doing what you asked them to do. Analyze your strengths and weaknesses in relation to both verbal limit-setting and positive verbal assertions.

3. How effectively do you assertively follow through

on your verbal responses? If your words are not sufficient to influence the student's behavior, how well do you follow through with appropriate consequences? Again, evaluate yourself in two distinct aspects, limit-setting consequences and positive consequences. In other words, if you tell a child to get to work and he won't, how well do you back up your words with consequences (i.e., "Do your work now or you will choose to do it after school!")? Or, if your praise is not sufficient to motivate a student, how well do you again back up your words with appropriate consequences (i.e., "If you work quietly you can earn a positive note to your parents.")?

4. How effectively do you plan how you will deal with the behavior of your students? How well do you plan your discipline efforts with your students? Do you systematically plan how you will prevent behavior problems from developing? Do you systematically plan how you will eliminate behavior problems when they do occur? If your initial discipline efforts are not successful, do you systematically plan how to change them in order to increase their effectiveness? (See *Assertive Discipline Plan*, p. 145.)

It will be useful to spend time each day coding how you typically respond to your students. You may want to take notes on a pad, or possibly tape record yourself for a brief part of the day. Once this is done and you have an idea of your strengths and weaknesses, you will be in a position to determine what specific changes you will need to make in order to become more assertive in your classroom. Here are some examples of what we mean.

"I need to stop ignoring the children's shouting out, clearly let them know I want it to stop, and be prepared to follow through if they don't."

"I need to start letting the children know more often that I like it when they do their work on time."

"I have to stop pleading or screaming when the children get out of their seats. Instead, I need finally to let them know I want them to sit there, or I will discipline them. As well, I need to let them know I like it when they do stay seated."

"I have to demonstrate to the children through my words and actions that I am the 'boss.' I need to set limits whenever they disrupt. I need also to give them positive attention when they are quiet."

"I need to stop telling the children over and over what I want. I need to follow through on my words more."

"I have to start planning how I'm going to deal with problems, before they get out of hand."

"I have to stop sounding like a Drill Sergeant barking out an order to the students. I have to start becoming more positive when they do what I want."

Finally, it is necessary for many teachers to repeat this same analysis of their behavior, this time in relation to how they deal with specific "powerful children" in their class. In many instances a teacher who is verbally assertive with the majority of her students may be verbally non-assertive with certain difficult students. Or, a teacher may follow-through assertively with all of her students except for those she is not comfortable in confronting.

5

VERBAL
LIMIT-SETTING

Now, let's focus on your developing more assertive responses to the children's behavior. We are going to begin with assertive limit-setting, for we believe a teacher must feel she has the *influence* to help the students eliminate inappropriate, problem behavior. Until a teacher feels she has this influence, we feel she will not be comfortable enough with her students to provide them the meaningful warmth and support they need. In other words, it is hard to be nice to students who you are afraid will "tear" your class apart!

The first approach to limit-setting is verbal (i.e., "saying what you mean, and meaning what you say"). The initial aspect of verbal limit-setting is to determine how you will verbally request specific behavior on the part of the children. There are four general methods of requesting behavior:

HINTS
"Everyone should be working."

QUESTIONS
"Would you please get to work."

I MESSAGES
"I want you to open your books and get to work."

DEMANDS
"Get to work now."

Whenever possible, utilize a "hint," a "question," or an "I message" to request the behavior you desire. This is important because, first, most children will respond immediately to them, and, second, a demand differs from these three in a significant manner. A demand implies a consequence for non-compliance, "get to work now, or else . . . !" Unfortunately, we know that all too often teachers will make a demand when they in no way mean to, or are in no way prepared to, follow-through with a consequence for non-compliance. This often results in the teacher responding non-assertively, and teaching the students to disregard her words. Here is an example of exactly what we mean:

Teacher: "O.K., class. It's time to get to work on your math. (All of the students get to work except Mark, who constantly disregards his teacher's direction.)

Teacher: "Mark, I was talking to you, too. Get to work now!"

Mark: "I will, I will." (Mark continues to play with papers on his desk.)

Teacher: "Mark, get to work!"

Mark: (Takes out work, but begins to talk to his neighbor.)

Teacher (even louder): "Look, I don't want to have to talk to you again. Get to work!"

Mark: (Stops talking but does not get to work.)

Teacher (angrily): "If I have to talk to you one more time, you've had it!"

Mark: (Looks at his work, but soon begins to play with the rubber bands in his desk.)

Teacher (frustratedly): "Mark, I will not tolerate this any longer, I've had it. Get to work!"

Mark: (Picks up a pencil and stares blankly at the paper. As soon as the teacher walks away, he again begins to play with his rubber bands.)

The students of this teacher, especially Mark, through exchanges like this, will learn quickly not to listen to their teacher's demands. As a result, the teacher probably will resort to hostile screaming, name calling, or physically grabbing the students to get her requests met.

The first, and only, Commandment of *Assertive Discipline* is this: *"Thou shalt not make a demand thou art not preparest to follow-through upon!"* For the sake of your students and yourself, do not make a demand unless you are prepared to follow-through. Before you go to a student and deliver a demand, ask yourself this one question: *What am I prepared to do if the child does not comply with my demand?* If you have a response ready that is both appropriate and assertive, then you are ready to make your demand. If you don't have a response, plan one, then make your demand. Or, if you can't think of an appropriate response, wait until you have one before you make a demand that you cannot enforce.

Back to the example of Mark and his not working, here is how the teacher could have dealt with him assertively:

Teacher: "Mark, I was talking to you, too. Get to work now!"

Mark: "I will, I will." (Mark continues to play with paper.)

Teacher (firmly):   "Mark, you have a choice: Get to work now, or you will have to do the work after school."

To recapitulate, these are the points we want you to remember: (1) use a "hint," a "question," or an "I message" whenever they are effective (the less you have to use demands, the more effective they will be!); (2) don't make demands you can't follow through on.

In relation to verbal limit-setting, *how* you state what you want is as important as *what* you say. You communicate just as much through your tone of voice and non-verbal behavior as you do with your words. Learning how to deliver an effective message is a significant step in developing assertive verbal skills. Note closely *how* the teacher in the following example delivered her request:

> The teacher observed Steve roughly pushing and shoving the children standing beside him in line. The teacher walked up to Steve, *looked him in the eyes, placed her hand on his shoulder,* and stated, "Steve, keep your hands to yourself!" *(while gesturing with her free hand).*

Eye contact, gestures, use of name, and touch, are all useful in increasing the effectiveness of your verbal communication. To help you learn how to use these skills, we have developed a simple exercise. Find another individual to try this exercise with. Sit, or stand, and face one another. You begin by sending the message "stop disrupting" according to the directions that will follow. Then you reverse the roles and receive the message from your partner. Go through all of the steps first, then repeat them.

1: Say "stop disrupting" while looking *over* your partner's shoulder. Make sure not to make eye contact.

2. Say "stop disrupting" *looking* your partner right in the eye.

3. Say "stop disrupting," gesturing with your hand towards your partner, while still looking her in the eye.

4. Include your partner's first name before your demand, i.e., "Susan, stop disrupting." Continue to gesture and use eye contact.

5. Utilize all aspects of #4—eye contact, gesturing, and first name—but, this time put your other hand on your partner's shoulder.

6. Repeat #1—looking over your shoulder.

7. Repeat #5—eye contact, pointing, name, hand on shoulder.

As you do this exercise, you will clearly experience the significance of the following aspects of communication.

Eye Contact: When you deliver a message without making eye contact, your message will be ineffective. Eye contact is vital to human communication. We say as much with our eyes as our words. You can increase the effectiveness of any message by looking the other individual (e.g., student, parent, principal) in the eye when you speak. Whenever possible, make eye contact with a student when telling him what you want.

Hand Gesture: Gestures are utilized to emphasize our words. You may note that, during the exercise, when you say "stop disrupting" while using hand gestures, your voice becomes firmer and naturally more forceful. Hand gestures non-verbally communicate, "I mean what I am saying."

An important point to remember: There is a major difference between a hand gesture designed to emphasize your words, and hand gestures designed to intimidate a child. Namely, we are referring to shaking your finger in the child's face as you speak. This does little more than to frighten a child, and is basically hostile.

Name: Using a child's name, when delivering a message, personalizes the message, thus increasing its impact. It is particularly significant to use children's names when they are not in close proximity to you. For example, when children across the room are making a disturbance, rather than stating, "You kids in the corner, stop talking so loud," state, "Mark, Sue, and Steve, stop talking so loud." There is no doubt in the latter statement to whom you were specifically directing your comments.

Touch: Physical touch adds the impact of creating physical as well as verbal limits. Placing your hand on a child, when you speak to him, is a clear indicator of the sincerity and forcefulness of your message. For some children, your hand on their shoulder will communicate more than any words you could say.

A few quick notes on the non-verbal aspects we have discussed. Some children will not want to look you in the eye. This may be due to a number of reasons, including fear, defiance, or culturally learned behavior. You have to decide if it is, or isn't, appropriate to make the child look at you by gently turning his eyes towards you. Also, some children do not like to be touched; thus, putting your hand on their shoulder may just unduly provoke them in a way you don't want. Again, we are not giving you absolutes in how to deal with each and every situation. You are a professional, and you need to use your knowledge and skills in evaluating each situation as to how you can most effectively deal with it.

Verbally setting limits in an assertive manner requires you to be able to "say what you mean, and mean what you say." It requires you to be able to *persist* in your verbal demands as well. By persist, we mean being capable of stating what your wants are, over and over again, without getting sidetracked by the students. We often work with teachers who initially state their wants clearly and firmly, but who get manipulated many times by the responses of their students.

> **Teacher:** "Sue, I want you to raise your hand and wait to be called upon before you speak." (statement of want)
>
> **Sue:** "None of the other children do."
>
> **Teacher:** "What do you mean, none of the other children do?"
>
> **Sue:** "Kevin always shouts out."
>
> **Teacher:** "When?"
>
> **Sue:** "He did it all morning during our social studies discussion."
>
> **Teacher:** "I'll take care of Kevin, don't worry."
>
> **Sue:** "Well, even if I raise my hand you never call on me."
>
> **Teacher** (getting frustrated): "Yes, I do."
>
> **Sue:** "You didn't this morning."
>
> **Teacher** (even more frustrated): "Look, Sue, I don't want to talk about this any more, you just don't listen to me."

In this example, you can observe how Sue was able to manipulate the teacher verbally. The teacher did not stick to her wants (i.e., "Raise your hand and wait to be called upon before you speak"). She ended up dealing with Sue's "sidetracking" responses (e.g., "Kevin shouts out" or "you don't call on me"). When this occurs, the students, in effect, take control of the interchange, thus preventing the teacher from meeting her own needs and the realistic needs of the students.

We have found an effective way to persist verbally in your wants with your students. It is called *The Broken Record.* The Broken Record is derived directly from *Assertion Training.* The Broken Record gets its name from the fact that when you utilize it, you end up sounding like a broken or stuck record, which keeps repeating the same statement over, and over, and. . . . When you learn to speak as if you were a broken record, you will be capable of expressing your wants and needs, and ignore all sidetracking manipulations of the students. Back to the example of Sue:

Teacher: "Sue, I want you to raise your hand and wait to be called upon before you speak." (statement of want)

Sue: "None of the other children do."

Teacher: "That's not the point, I want you to raise your hand." (Broken Record)

Sue: "You never call on me."

Teacher: "That's not the point, I want you to raise your hand." (Broken Record)

Sue: "O.K., I will."

In this interchange, the teacher simply kept repeating (Broken Record) what she wanted from the child, and would not become sidetracked by Sue's responses. The teacher maintained control of the interaction with the child.

In utilizing a Broken Record, you first need to determine what you want from the interaction with the student (i.e., "I want Sue to raise her hand"). This becomes your *statement of want* and the gist of your interactions.

You can preface your statement of want with "That's not the point" ("... I want you to raise your hand"), or "I understand, but ..." ("... I want you to raise your hand"). No matter what manipulative response the student presents, if you respond with your statement of want—That's not the point, I want you to ... ," or "I understand, but I want you to ..."—your statement will be more effective. Also, when delivering your statement of want, always remember to utilize appropriate eye contact, gestures, the child's name, and touch, to add impact to your message.

In most instances, when using a Broken Record you will need to repeat your statement of want to the student a maximum of three times.

> **Teacher:**   "Craig, I want you to start your project now." (statement of want)
>
> **Craig:**   "I will as soon as I finish my game. Just a few more minutes."
>
> **Teacher** (firmly):   "Craig, I understand, but I want you to start your project now." (Broken Record)
>
> **Craig:**   "You never give me enough time with the games."
>
> **Teacher** (calmly, firmly):   "That's not the point, I want you to start your project now."
>
> **Craig:**   "I don't like doing my project."
>
> **Teacher** (firmly):   "I understand, but I want you to start your project."
>
> **Craig:**   "Wow, you really mean it. I'll get to work."

What if Craig still would not get to work? What if you

repeated your statement three times and the child said, "so what?" As with any demand, you need to be prepared with the follow-through consequences to support your words. Back to the example of Craig. What if Craig's final response to the teacher was "I won't do my project!" The teacher then would need to reinforce her words with a consequence: "Craig, you have a choice—work on your project now, or you will have to work on it after school!"

When utilizing a Broken Record, or whenever you are verbally setting limits with students, it is imperative that you remain as *calm* as possible—no matter how the students may try to provoke you. Don't fight or argue with the students—don't scream or yell your demands at them—verbalize your wants in as firm and calm a tone of voice as possible. Many students will do anything to provoke and upset you. They do this, for they have learned that the more upset a teacher becomes, the easier it is to manipulate or sidetrack her. Don't forget it takes two people to have a "fight." If you are not willing to "fight" with students, it will make it much more difficult for them to "create a scene" in the classroom.

The benefit of using a Broken Record is that it will help you to remain calm and maintain the focus on your wants and needs, rather than on the manipulations of the students. It will also enable you to respond in a manner the students are not accustomed to. Students are used to teachers being sidetracked by their verbal manipulations, manipulations which teachers should be aware of. Here are examples of typical manipulations that students engage in to sidetrack teachers. Note how teachers typically (non-assertively) respond to the manipulations, and finally, how teachers can respond assertively.

"You Don't Like Me"

Steve is a very aggressive child who refuses to take responsibility for his actions. Whenever his teacher confronted him about his fighting he blamed everyone else, either for provoking him into fighting or for blaming him unfairly.

Teacher: "Steve, I will not tolerate your fighting with your peers. You will stop fighting in this class." (statement of want)

Steve: "It's not my fault. The children pick on me."

Teacher: "That's not true, you start the fights."

Steve: "You don't like me. You're like everyone else who picks on me."

Teacher: "Steve, I do like you. If I didn't, I would not be here now."

Steve: "If you liked me, you would believe that I was right, that the other children pick on me."

Teacher: "I want to believe you, but it's hard. You get into so many fights. Look, to show you that I really do like you, and that I am trying to believe you, I'll give you another chance."

The child "sidetracked" the teacher from the demand of "stop fighting" and into trying to prove to the child that he really is cared about. An assertive teacher may respond to the same child as follows:

Teacher (with eye contact, hand on shoulder): "Steve, I will not tolerate your fighting. You will stop fighting in this class!" (statement of want)

Steve: "It's not my fault. They pick on me."

Teacher (firmly): "That's not the point, you will stop fighting in this class!"

Steve: "You don't like me. You are like everybody else who picks on me."

Teacher (firmly): "I understand, but you will stop fighting in this class!"

Steve: "You're just picking on me. I'll do what I want!"

Teacher (calmly): "Steve, you will stop fighting. You have a choice: you may stop fighting, or I will call your parents every time you fight!"

Steve: "Wow, you just want to get me in trouble!"

Teacher (calmly): "Steve, it's your choice. When you choose to fight, then you also choose to have me call your parents!"

"Crying"

Carol is a very immature child. Unless she gets her way she will disrupt the class. Whenever the teacher attempts to deal with Carol, she immediately breaks down and cries. This takes place almost on a daily basis.

Teacher: "Carol, I want you to stop poking and shoving the children who sit next to you on the rug. It will stop now!" (statement of want)

Carol (beginning to cry): "But I didn't mean to do it."

Teacher: "Now, now, Carol. No need to get so upset. Every time I talk to you about your behavior you cry."

Carol (sobbing): "I'm sorry."

Teacher: "Carol, it's okay. I'm not angry with you. Just calm down. Here, blow your nose. We can talk when you are calmer. You're just having a rough day."

No one likes to see a child cry. No one likes to feel she made a child cry. Some children, such as Carol, quickly learn that if they get upset and cry, the teacher will feel guilty and stop placing demands on them. An assertive teacher may respond to Carol in this manner:

Teacher (eye contact, firmly): "I want you to stop poking and shoving the children that are sitting next to you." (statement of want)

Carol (beginning to cry): "But I didn't mean to."

Teacher (firmly): "That's not the point, I want you to stop poking and shoving the children who sit next to you!"

Carol (sobbing): "But I didn't mean to."

Teacher (calmly): "I understand, but I don't want you to poke and shove the children who sit next to you!"

Carol (stops crying): "All right, I'll keep my hands to myself."

"Belligerence"

Matt does not do his classwork. When confronted about this, he becomes volatile in his response, a response he has learned to be effective in manipulating his teachers.

Teacher: "Matt, I will not put up with your refusing to do your work. You will do your work in this class." (statement of want)

Child: "I don't give a darn what you say. You can't make me!"

Teacher (fuming): "Don't you talk to me that way, who do you think you are?"

Child: "Who do you think *you* are?"

Teacher (yelling): "Listen, young man, I'm not going to take this from you."

Child: "I don't give a darn what you do."

Teacher (yelling): "You are disgusting. You'll be sorry for what you're saying. I won't tolerate children talking to me this way. Get out of here!"

The teacher allowed the child's anger to "hook" her. She was responding to the child's hostility rather than persisting that the child do his work. The teacher, thus, did not get her needs met. An assertive teacher may respond as follows.

Teacher: "Matt, I will not put up with your refusing to work. You will do your work in this class." (statement of want)

Matt: "I don't give a darn what you say. You can't make me."

Teacher (calmly, firmly): "Matt, you will do your work in this class!" (Broken Record)

Matt: "If you want your work done—you do it!"

Teacher (calmly): "Matt, you will do your work in this class—or I will call your parents. It is your choice." (follow-through consequence)

Matt: "You just want to get me in trouble!"

Teacher: "That's not the point, you have a choice: You will choose to do your work in class—or you will choose to have me call your parents." (Broken Record, follow-through)

Matt: "I won't do my work."

Teacher (calmly): "Okay. You have chosen to have your parents called. I will call them at recess!"

"I'm Sorry—Give Me Another Chance"

Sue Ann has learned to get around limits by quickly apologizing for her actions and making promises never to do it again. The problem with such a child is that her apologies and promises are not sincere, for she continues to engage in the same inappropriate behavior.

Teacher: "Sue Ann, I will not put up with your leaving a mess every time you paint. You will clean up after yourself." (statement of want)

Sue Ann: "I'm sorry, Ms. C., please forgive me."

Teacher: "That's what you *always* say."

Sue Ann: "I know I've been wrong. I'll be good."

Teacher: "You promised last week to be good, and yet, you made a mess again today."

Sue Ann: "I've been really tired lately. I mean it this time. I'll be good, I swear I will."

Teacher: "Okay, one last chance. From now on, I want to see some real effort out of you."

Once again, the teacher did not persist in her demands with the child. The child was able to sidetrack her with promises and apologies. The teacher did not want apologies—she wanted the child to stop making a mess. An assertive teacher could have responded as follows:

Teacher: "Sue Ann, I will not put up with your leaving a mess every time you paint. You will clean up after yourself!" (statement of want)

Sue Ann: "I'm sorry, Ms. C., please forgive me."

Teacher: "That's not the point. You will clean up after yourself!"

Sue Ann: "I've been really tired lately. I'm sorry."

Teacher (firmly):   "I understand, but you will clean up after yourself!"

Sue Ann: "I hear what you are saying. I will clean up after myself."

In each of these examples, when the teachers responded assertively they did not become sidetracked or "hooked" by the child's guilt-provoking statements, anger, tears, or promises. They were able to maintain the focus on their wants and persisted in stating them calmly and firmly.

How does it feel to use a Broken Record? One previously non-assertive teacher described it this way:

"I rarely felt as if I could get my point across to my students unless I ranted and raved. The first time I used a Broken Record was with a little 'toughie,' Leon, who would not remain in his seat. He was up and down constantly, bugging the students around him in the process. Finally, one day I was out of patience. During some lesson, I don't remember which one, he got up and began to wander around the room. I thought to myself, now is the time to see if that Broken Record will really work. I walked up to him, looked him right in the eye, placed my hand firmly on his shoulder, and said, 'Leon, you will sit down now!' He quickly came back with something like, 'I'm tired of working.' I said to myself, don't respond to his remark, repeat your want. So I said, 'That's not the point, Leon, you will sit down now!' He became angry and said something to the effect that I was picking on him. I remained cool and repeated my demand, 'Leon, that's not the point, you will sit down now!' The third time was a charm! He looked at me with a shocked expression, and said simply, 'Okay, I will.' Then he went to his seat and got to work. To say the least, I was surprised at how effective I had been with him. I realized, then, how I had allowed the children to take advantage of me. I could get my needs met if I kept them in focus and communicated them firmly and consistently to the children."

In summary, we would like to review how to utilize the Broken Record:

1. Determine your statement of want in the interaction.

2. Preface the statement with "That's not the point, . . ." or "I understand, but. . . ."

3. Respond to any sidetracking responses with your statement of want.

4. Utilize a Broken Record a maximum of three times.

5. When delivering your message, utilize appropriate eye contact, gestures, touch, etc.

6. Be prepared with a follow-through consequence, if appropriate.

A Broken Record is a highly useful assertive skill. It can be abused! The Broken Record is designed to be utilized only in interactions with children who: (1) refuse to listen to you; (2) persist in responding inappropriately to your demands (e.g., cry, scream, talk back); and/or (3) refuse to take responsibility for their own behavior. Children may have legitimate reasons why they cannot comply with your requests, in which case, you will accomplish nothing by droning on "That's not the point . . ." in response to their statements.

6

LIMIT-SETTING
FOLLOW-THROUGH:

A PROMISE NOT A THREAT

Follow-through is essential to assertive limit-setting. For many children, especially those in a "power struggle" with a teacher, "actions speak louder than words." In order to assert your influence effectively, it often is necessary to demonstrate your sincerity by reinforcing your verbal requests or demands with appropriate consequences. We are not saying, for example, that you should run around your class continuously telling the children to "sit down or I will call your mother." What we are saying, and have said, is that you should have consequences ready to back up your words when it is necessary and appropriate.

Assertive teachers "promise" rather than "threaten" to follow-through on their verbal requests. A "promise" is a vow of affirmative action. A "threat" is a statement or expression of intention to hurt or punish. Assertive teachers "promise" to follow-through, because they are aware that providing needed limit-setting consequences is an affirmative action which benefits the student. Assertive teachers are also aware that to allow students to engage in inappropriate, self-destructive behavior is essentially a "threat" to a student's well-being, and in the long run it is the most severe punishment that can be inflicted upon a student.

Even though effective limit-setting is an affirmative action which benefits students, we know of no teacher who enjoys setting limits! No teacher, especially an assertive one, likes the stress and discomfort which is inherent in the limit-setting process. We cannot imagine a teacher being elated about the fact that she found it necessary to keep students in from lunch or after school!, send them to the principal, or call their parents. We cannot imagine a teacher being elated when her students angrily call her "mean" or "unfair," "beg for mercy," cry, or have a tantrum, as a direct result of her limit-setting actions. In being assertive, teachers recognize that limit-setting is an unpleasant, yet essential, responsibility of their position in the classroom.

An integral aspect of limit-setting follow-through is *choice*. Limit-setting consequences need to be "spelled out" to the students so that they can make the choice as to whether the consequences will occur.

> **Teacher:** "Carl, I want you to keep your hands to yourself. If you poke someone you will *choose* to sit by yourself at the table. It's your choice!"
>
> **Carl:** "Okay." (However, he gradually begins to poke the children around him.)
>
> **Teacher:** "Carl, you poked Fred and Sue, you have *chosen* to sit by yourself at the table."

When we provide the students with the choice as to whether the limit-setting consequence will occur, we place the responsibility where it belongs—on the students. They are the ones who choose to poke the other children; thus, they are the ones who choose to sit by themselves. When we provide a student with a choice, we are providing him with the opportunity to learn the natural consequence of his inappropriate actions, and that he is responsible for his behavior.

> **Teacher:** "Karen, you will stop talking and do your work—or you will choose to spend the rest of the period working in the office. It's your choice."
>
> **Karen:** "I hear you, I hear you." (starts working for a few minutes, but soon begins talking loudly again)

Teacher: "Karen, you are talking. Therefore, it is your choice to go to the office. Now take your work and go into the office."

Karen: "I'm sorry. I don't want to go."

Teacher: "Karen, you were talking and, thus, made your own choice."

Karen: "Please don't make me go. I want to do my work in here."

Teacher: "I understand, but it was your choice. Tomorrow you can choose to do your work in here."

By allowing the child to choose if the limit-setting consequences will occur, you simultaneously place your role in the proper perspective—you no longer become the "bad guy" who gets the child in trouble. Karen did not have to go to the office, she *chose* to go. Carl did not have to sit by himself, he *chose* to. A student may choose to have his parents called, go to the principal, or receive detention—the choice becomes part of his responsibility. However, it is your responsibility to (1) let the students clearly know the behaviors you do not want, (2) let the students know clearly what consequences they will choose if they engage in the inappropriate behaviors, and (3) make sure they receive the consequences they choose.

We have mentioned the need for effective follow-through consequences. Here are the basic criteria we have found useful in determining the consequences to be used. In order to follow-through meaningfully on your demands, you will want to utilize a consequence which is:

1.   One you are comfortable using (i.e., don't keep the

child after school unless you don't mind staying after with him).

2. Something the child does not like, but is not physically or psychologically harmful.

3. Provided to the child as a choice.

4. Provided as soon as possible after the child chooses to disregard your request (i.e., immediately send the child to the corner, or immediately tell the child "a note will be going home").

5. Provided in a matter-of-fact manner, without hostile screaming or yelling (i.e., "You did not do your work—you chose not to have free time").

6. Provided every time the child disregards your limits. The message you send to the child is, again: "I care too much about you as an individual to allow you to act in an inappropriate, self-destructive manner without doing all I can to help you to stop! I, as well, care too much about myself as a teacher and as an individual to allow you to take advantage of me, my wants, and my needs!"

The follow-through consequences you utilize are not as significant as how you use them. No consequence, be it as severe as suspension or as minimal as missing five minutes of free time, will influence a student's behavior unless you *persist* in using the consequence every time as indicated by the student's behavior.

Often in our workshops, teachers state, "Nothing will work with that child. I have tried everything—sending him to the principal, calling his parents, etc." Upon examination of the follow-through efforts of these teachers, we typically found something similar to the following had occurred:

1. The teacher was dealing with a difficult student who was often extremely disruptive.

2. The teacher tolerated a great deal of inappropriate behavior before finally following through with a consequence (i.e., calling the student's parents on a day when he was extremely disruptive).

3. The student's behavior dramatically improved after his parents were called. For the next two successive days he engaged in no inappropriate behavior.

4. The third day after the call to his parents he engaged in two disruptive outbursts, which the teacher responded to non-assertively (i.e., "tolerating" the behavior). When the teacher was asked why the parents were not called again, she stated, "He is so much better, those outbursts were nothing."

5. The next day, the student engaged in three outbursts—the following day, four outbursts. Again she was asked why she had not called the parents, and she replied, "His behavior is still much better than before. He is not 'so bad' that I need to call his mom."

6. From the sixth day on the student engaged in four to five outbursts per day. This total was just below the number of outbursts which resulted in the first call to his parents (six). The teacher did not call this time, because she felt, "It won't do any good. He's just as bad as he was before I called!"

Calling the parents *was* an effective limit-setting follow-through consequence. It was effective because it influenced the student to eliminate his outbursts for two days. If it could influence the child to choose to eliminate the behavior for two days, then it could influence him for a longer period of time. The key, again, is the persistent use of the consequence (calling the parents). The follow-through effort did not work because the teacher allowed the student's outbursts to continue too long without providing a consequence. For the teacher to be effective, she needed to call the parents on the third day, when the student engaged in two outbursts. Also, she needed to respond persistently each time he chose to act inappropriately, since choosing to act inappropriately meant choosing to have his parents called. In reality, "nothing will work" when the teacher does not persistently utilize the follow-through consequences available to her!

Speaking realistically, some consequences are not effective with certain students, no matter how persistently they are used. Some students would not mind missing recess or having to sit in the corner. In these cases, when following through with a specific consequence, use the same consequence three times in succession whenever the student engages in the same inappropriate behavior. If, however, the student continues to engage in the behavior, it is necessary to find and utilize an additional consequence, as was the case with Madeline:

Teacher: "Madeline, if you continue to talk out without raising your hand, you will choose to miss five minutes of your recess."

Madeline: "Okay."

Teacher (begins lesson).

Madeline (without raising hand): "I don't like this dumb history."

Teacher: "Madeline, you talked out—you have chosen to lose five minutes of your recess."

Madeline (without raising her hand): "I don't care! This lesson stinks."

Teacher: "Madeline, you have now chosen to lose ten minutes of recess!"

Madeline (without raising her hand): "Why do I have to do this lesson? I hate history!"

Teacher: "Madeline, that's now 15 minutes off your recess!"

Madeline (without raising her hand): "I don't care if I never go to recess—I don't like this boring history!"

If, after following through again with a consequence three times, the child continues to engage in the inappropriate behavior, it is necessary to implement an additional consequence. Typically, this new consequence should be one that is more severe.

Teacher: "Madeline, you have a choice: if you talk out again you will not only lose 15 minutes of your recess but you will be sent to the principal's office!"

Madeline: (not wanting to go to the principal's office, chooses to participate appropriately in the lesson.)

LIMIT-SETTING CONSEQUENCES

Let's get to the specific follow-through limit-setting consequences that you will find useful. We will begin with the most common consequences that teachers utilize. They are in all probability consequences you have used with your own students. We will then present three additional consequences that we have found useful in dealing with behavior problems.

Time Out: More commonly known as "isolation." The child has to sit in an isolated corner for 10 to 20 minutes. This works best with younger children.

Removal of a Privilege or Positive Activity: Take away free time, recess, P.E., monitory privileges, or a field trip, etc. Be sure it's an activity that is meaningful to the child, and one he would not want to miss.

Stay After School (Detention): The child has to stay after school in the classroom, principal's office, etc. This is particularly effective with children who do not complete their work during class time. The consequence for their behavior is to stay after school and complete their work.

Principal: The child is sent to sit in the principal's office or has to discuss the problem with the principal.

Home Consequences: Call or send a note home to the parents when the child acts inappropriately. Arrange for the parents to provide the child with a negative consequence at home, be it a lecture, no TV, or stay in bedroom. This is often the most effective consequence with many children.

The following are consequences we have found useful in assisting teachers to influence the behavior of more severe behavior problems. Since they may be new to you, we will discuss them in detail.

Time Out in Another Classroom:

This is a highly effective means of dealing with students who continuously refuse to behave in your classroom. When the student disrupts, he chooses to go and do his work in another classroom for half an hour or an hour. When implementing this consequence, you want to find a fellow teacher to whose class you can send the student. Be sure to choose a teacher who is known for good classroom management skills and who can control her own students. This consequence also is very useful for the following reasons:

You will always have somewhere to send the student. Your fellow teacher is in class and available whenever you need to utilize her. This is a more reliable arrangement than typically sending the student to a principal who may or may not be in his office and/or available to deal with the student. Both you and the student know that if he is sent to your peer's classroom he will have to sit and do his work for the predetermined length of time.

Students greatly dislike being removed from their class. They are not part of the new class, and they feel alienated. It is important to send the student to a class where he does not know many, if any, of the students (i.e., send a 4th grader to a 6th grade class). We never recommend sending students to a kindergarten room, since, for as long as we can remember, students have been humiliated by being sent "back to kindergarten." We do not send the students to another class to humiliate them. We send them there because they need to know that we will not tolerate their inappropriate behavior in our classroom!!!

Students will typically behave appropriately when placed in another teacher's classroom. When children are placed in an environment with which they are neither familiar nor comfortable, they will usually behave appropriately. First, they will not know how the other teacher will respond, and second, they will not have their classmates to encourage their inappropriate behavior. Rarely have we heard of a student who was timed out in another classroom disrupting the second class!

This is an easy consequence to demonstrate effectively to the student. Before you implement the consequence, you can have the student go with you to the other teacher's class, and both you and your peer can show him where he will sit and do his work. Your peer, as well, can firmly tell him how she expects him to behave in the class.

This is an easy consequence to utilize. When the student disrupts, you can simply have him take his work and go to the other classroom. When his time is up, the other teacher can send him back. If he again disrupts and chooses to go back, back he goes! Here is an example of the successful use of time out in another classroom:

Allan was a 3rd grader in Mr. C.'s class who was highly, and we mean highly, disruptive. During work time he frequently would get out of his seat and talk to and bother the other children. When the children were on the rug, he would constantly squirm around and poke and push the children near him. During transitions between activities he would get very loud and often would run around the room.

Mr. C. had attempted to work with Allan's parents, but they were in the process of getting a divorce and were not cooperative at all. He had attempted to reinforce Allan's positive behavior by providing Allan extra time with him whenever Allan did not disrupt. This did not work, nor did sending Allan to the corner for ten minutes when he disrupted. When in the corner, Allan made more noise than ever. Mr. C. finally decided in order to deal assertively with Allan, he would need to time Allan out in another room.

He met with Ms. M., whose 6th grade class was across the hall, and explained the situation to her. Ms. M. agreed to have Allan come to her room and sit in the corner and do his work when needed. They *both* then met with Allan.

Mr. C.: "Allan, I will not tolerate your getting out of your seat, poking and pushing the children on the rug, or running and yelling in the classroom. This will stop! If you engage in any of those behaviors you will choose to go to Ms. M.'s class and work alone in the back of the room for half an hour."

Allan: "I don't want to go to her room!"

Mr. C.: "I understand, Allan, but it's your choice if you go or stay."

Ms. M.: "Allan, if you choose to come to my room you will sit in the seat in the corner by the bookcase and do your work with no talking. When your half hour is up I will tell you, and then you may walk back to class."

Mr. C.: "Allan, I want to be sure you understand what we are saying to you. Tell us what you have heard."

Allan: "When I act bad I go to Ms. M.'s room and work."

Mr. C.: "What do you mean by 'bad'?"

Allan: "When I get up and bother the other kids, play around and push them on the rug, or scream and yell and run in the room."

Mr. C.: "That's right. Now, we will start this plan today."

Allan acted appropriately that entire day after the meeting. The next day he acted up on the rug, totally disrupting a story. Mr. C. told him that he had chosen to go to Ms. M.'s class and do his work for half an hour. Mr. C.

left the class with an aide and escorted Allan across the hall. Ms. M. greeted Allan and took him to his seat. Her students had been told that if any students from another class came to work in their classroom they were to pay no attention to them. Allan immediately got to work, and, as typically occurs, was no problem at all while he was in the strange classroom. When the half hour was up Allan returned to his classroom. Upon entering he told Mr. C. that he "hated it in Ms. M.'s room and never wanted to go back." Mr. C. reiterated that it had been Allan's choice to go. Allan chose to go one more time that week. For Allan the second time was the charm—two visits to Ms. M.'s class were sufficient to motivate him to eliminate his disruptive behavior.

Tape Recording Behavior:

Tape recording a student's behavior and playing it for his parents or the principal is a significant consequence for a child. We would *only* use it, though, in select situations, such as (1) when the parents will not believe "their child" is actually the problem we say he is, or (2) when all else fails. We will only tape record the student with his full knowledge, and the parents' approval. *Under no circumstances* will we play the tape for anyone but the school personnel or the parents! We are not taping the student to spy on him; instead, we want the tape as a record of his behavior to share with specific adults. The goal of this consequence is to acquire the cooperation of others in helping the student to eliminate his inappropriate behavior. Taping is a useful consequence for these reasons:

It is an easy consequence to utilize. Simply put a tape

recorder by the child and turn it on. If the child was disruptive during the taping, play the tape for the principal and/or parents.

Students react strongly to being taped. They already know that their behavior is inappropriate and disruptive. They are not proud of it—and definitely do not want others to hear how they act in class. Many problem students immediately shape up the minute the recorder is turned on, and their behavior remains appropriate as long as the tape is running. After a while, most students will choose to act in an appropriate manner if you just mention to them that you will tape them again if they continue to act inappropriately.

It can convince reluctant parents and principals that positive action needs to be taken with the student. When parents actually hear their child talking back to the teacher, refusing to work, cursing and screaming, they usually become supportive of you and your efforts in assisting their child.

The following is an example of a successful use of taping:

Murry was an immature 8th grader. He believed that all teachers were out to get him, and therefore picked on him obsessively. When his teacher, Mr. F., demanded he do his work, Murry would become upset and accuse Mr. F. of picking on him. Murry could be very convincing in his actions—so convincing that he had his mother believing everything he said. As a result, the mother had been uncooperative with the school in their attempts to deal with Murry's problems.

Mr. F. felt that in order to meet his and Murry's needs, he had to have the cooperation of Murry's mother. To do this, he decided to tape Murry's behavior in the classroom.

He called the mother and explained what he was planning to do. The mother could not believe that Mr. F. was going to so much trouble, but she agreed that she would like to hear what actually occurred in the classroom. Mr. F. then sat down with Murry and explained what he was going to do.

Mr. F.: "Murry, I will not tolerate your refusing to work. You will do your work! I have here a tape recorder, and I am going to place it by your seat and turn it on. It will record your behavior throughout the period. If you disrupt, and/or refuse to work, it will be on the tape. I have spoken to your mother and she will come in to hear the tape if you choose to have this occur."

Murry: "You are really going to record my behavior? You're kidding!"

Mr. F.: "No, I'm not. You will choose whether or not your mother has to hear the tapes."

Murry: "All she would hear is you picking on me, that's all!"

Mr. F. (calmly): "The recorder will be in effect today. It's your choice if your mother hears the tape!"

Murry did his work without incident for three straight days. On the fourth day he was in a bad mood and did not want to work. When Mr. F. demanded he do his work, Murry replied, "I don't have to do my work. You can't make me! I don't care what you say, and I don't care if my 'old lady' hears this. She can't make me work, either!" Mr. F. called Murry's mother and arranged for a conference the next day. In the conference he played the tape. When the mother heard the tape she became livid. She looked her son in the eye and angrily stated, "Who do you think you are? You are going to stop these games. He's not picking on you. You just think you are a big man. Let me tell you this—you will do your work in school, or you will do it at home. You will not leave the house or watch T.V. until your work is done. I've been a sucker for your act too long! Your game is over, whether you like it or not!" To say the least, Murry heard his mother. His behavior improved dramatically from that day on!

Systematic Exclusion:

Systematic exclusion is an excellent consequence to use with severe problems if, and only if, you have the cooperation of both the principal and the parents. Whenever the child engages in any of the pre-specified behaviors, he chooses to be excluded from school for the rest of that day. When the child is excluded from school, the parents are expected to make sure that he spends the rest of the school day in his room completing his assigned work. Systematic exclusion needs to be highly structured. The student must know exactly which behaviors will result in his being excluded from school. The teacher must have a specific plan prepared with regard to how the parents will be notified that they need to come get their child. And, the parents must be available to complete the follow-through. In most instances, it is advisable for the teacher, parents, and principal to write the details of the plan to make sure that all of the issues are clear and that there will be no misinterpretations.

Systematic exclusion is effective because:

It clearly demonstrates to the student that his teacher and parents are working together.

Very few students enjoy being excluded from school and spending the rest of the day sitting in their room.

**It enables the teacher to get systematic support from
parents with regard to setting limits with a difficult
student.**

Here is an example of the successful use of systematic
exclusion:

> Carl was a very aggressive 3rd grader who was involved
> daily in verbal and physical confrontations with his class-
> mates. Because of his large size, he was able to intimidate
> the other children. On two occasions, he had extorted
> money from other students, using threats of physical
> harm. He was known as the "worst" kid in the school.
> Ms. S. had tried every approach possible to deal with his
> behavior. She had used positive reinforcement, kept him
> after school, and suspended him, etc., to no avail. Ms. S.
> met with her principal, and together they decided to ex-
> clude Carl from school whenever he did any of the follow-
> ing to another student: (1) threatened them, (2) cussed
> at them, (3) extorted money from them, or (4) physically
> assaulted them. Ms. S. and her principal then had a con-
> ference with Carl's parents. At the conference his parents
> were told, specifically, why systematic exclusion was
> needed, and how they could follow through at home. His
> parents voiced their support for Ms. S.'s approach to deal-
> ing with the problem. Carl was called into the conference,
> and together, Ms. S., his parents, and the principal told
> Carl the consequences he would receive if he chose to
> engage in any of the four specific inappropriate behaviors.
> As a final measure, and to insure that all issues were clar-
> ified, Ms. S. wrote down all of the details of the contract,
> had each person read it, and then had each sign it.
>   While participating in the conference, Carl had main-
> tained a belligerent "I don't care" attitude to everything
> that was being said and done.

The next day, on the way into the classroom, Carl got into an argument with another student and roughly shoved him. Ms. S. immediately went up to Carl and simply told him, "You pushed Sol. You have chosen to go home for the rest of the day!" Ms. S. contacted the office; the principal called Carl's mother, who came to get him. Carl went home and spent the rest of the school day in his room doing the work he would have done had he stayed in school.

The following day, during a spelling assignment, another student refused to let Carl copy his work, and Carl became angry. He threatened to beat the student up. Ms. S., hearing this, told Carl what he had done and that he would be going home again. His mother picked him up, and he spent the rest of the day at home in his room. Carl behaved appropriately for the next two days. On the third day, during free choice, Ms. S. observed him angrily cursing and screaming at a girl who would not give him a puzzle that she was playing with. Ms. S. repeated the same procedure of informing him of what he had done, and that by behaving inappropriately he had chosen to go home. For the first time Carl became upset. He began to cry and say that he did not want to go home. Ms. S. simply told him that he "had made a choice," and that he would be going home.

As was typical, the "third time was the charm." Ms. S.'s ability to deal assertively with Carl's behaviors let him know that his disruptions would not be tolerated. Carl thus chose to control his temper and behaved in an appropriate manner with his fellow students.

About this point in time you may be thinking, "Those consequences are fine for most students, but what about the student who really 'does not care.' What do you do?" The "I don't care" child is very difficult for many teachers to deal with. You are probably accustomed to children giving you "horrified" looks when you say they will be "going to the principal," or that you will "call their parents." If you are like many teachers, when a child says "So what, I don't care," you get a sinking feeling and say to yourself, "What am I going to do? Nothing works with that child!" *NOT TRUE!* The "I don't care child" is manipulating you! Such children have learned that such a response often sidetracks teachers and other adults from dealing with them effectively.

A classic example of this point was an 8th grade boy we worked with. He would frequently make cutting and obscene comments to his teacher. When his teacher told him that she would call his parents next time he made such comments he smirked and said, "So what? Big deal!" He was so cocky that he added, "Their phone number is 634–– – –." His teacher remained calm and did not fall for his manipulative actions. The next time he verbally abused her in class, she took him to the office to call his parents. On the way to the office he was his "I don't care," defiant self. He remained that way until the teacher placed the telephone receiver in his hand and told him to dial his parents to tell them what he said. The moment he realized she meant business, he broke down, crying, and begged her for another chance. Thankfully, his teacher asserted herself and had him call. His "I don't care" attitude ended that moment, and his behavior improved simultaneously.

Children may not care if you keep them after school once, suspend them every now and then, or send them to the corner infrequently. But, there are a few children who would not care if they knew that they would have to stay after school every day—they chose to, even if it meant five days straight. There are a few children who would not care if they knew they would be suspended every time they acted out, even if it meant three straight days of suspension. There are a few children who would not care if they knew you would send them to a corner for their inappropriate behavior every time they chose to go, even if it meant five times a day.

What we are trying to say is this: *If you really care, the children will really care. If you are prepared to use any means necessary and appropriate to influence the children to eliminate their inappropriate behavior they will sense your determination and quickly care about the consequences which they will have to face consistently if they choose to act inappropriately.*

We need to relate honestly our experience with teachers in relation to limit-setting follow-through. We know of few areas that cause as much difficulty for teachers as the effective planning and execution of follow-through consequences to back up limit-setting demands. Based on our experiences, teachers rarely prepare and plan the follow-through consequences for their demands in an organized and systematic manner. We cannot overemphasize the importance of a follow-through method which has been planned to the last detail and designed to handle whatever contingency that might arise.

One of our consultations perfectly illustrates the point we are trying to make. The consultation was concerned with a 6th grade teacher, Ms. L., and one of her children, Larry. Larry was a child with a very short temper, who would constantly have flare-ups when he would angrily refuse to do assignments that "he did not feel like doing." Ms. L. had been verbally assertive, and had reinforced Larry's positive behavior with extra free time, etc., to no avail. As we worked together, Ms. L. went through the following procedure for planning and implementing a follow-through program with Larry.

1. She focused on what she wanted Larry to do: complete his assignments without angry outbursts.

2. She carefully determined the follow-through consequences he would experience if he did not do what she asked: He would have to stay after school and finish his work. She felt this was an effective consequence since he liked going to the park and participating in the after-school recreation program. She also knew that the principal or vice-principal was usually at school until 4:30 p.m. and could possibly watch Larry while he worked.

3. She met with both the principal and vice-principal about Larry, and they agreed that they would be able to watch Larry until at least 4:30 p.m. She asked them to notify her, as soon as possible, if some problem prevented them from staying until that time on any day. She did this so that she could plan to stay late or find someone else to stay if they were not going to be available.

4. She then spoke with Larry's parents and explained the problems she was experiencing, and why she wanted to be able to keep him after school. She told them that she was sure that Larry would finish his work either in class or after school; but in case he didn't, she asked them to have him finish it at home. The parents agreed to the plan.

5. After the follow-through contingencies had been planned, she met with Larry. She told him (a) exactly what she wanted him to do, "Complete your assignments"; (b) what would happen if he didn't, "You will have to finish them after school in the principal's office"; and (c) why she was doing it, "I won't tolerate children not doing their work. I can't sit back and let you fail."

6. She followed through with her contingency and had

him stay *every day* that he chose not to do his work. The first day after she spoke to him, he did his work in class and thus did not have to stay after school. The next day, however, he did only half of his work and refused to do the rest. At the end of the school day she walked him to the principal's office. The principal was at a meeting, so she left him a note on the work that Larry had to complete. She also called Larry's mother to inform her that Larry would be at school and not at the park. It was necessary for him to go to the office for three out of the next four days. He always completed the work after school and never had to complete it at home.

On Monday of the second week, there was an emergency administrative meeting after school, which both the principal and vice-principal had to attend. As they had arranged, they let Ms. L. know that morning. Larry did not complete his math in the morning and, thus, had to stay after school. She thus changed her plans and arranged to stay with Larry after school.

That was the only day that week that Larry had to stay after school. The third week, he did not have to stay once. The fourth week, he had a rough day and, again, had to stay. That was the last time he had to stay after school for the rest of the year. As a result of Ms. L.'s efforts, Larry's work, as well as his temper, had greatly improved by the end of the semester.

Let's examine the specific principles involved in the planning and execution of this successful follow-through effort, principles which are *keys* to an effective follow-through with any child.

   1. *The teacher did not assume the behavior of others:* She did not assume the parents or the princi-

pal would cooperate with her plan—she personally spoke with each of them. She did not assume that the child would go to the office voluntarily—she took him each day.

2. *The teacher anticipated possible problems that might occur:* She prepared for the possibility that the child may not do his work after school—she planned further follow-through with the parents. She also prepared for the possibility of the principals' not being available—she asked them to notify her if this should occur.

3. *The teacher left nothing in doubt:* She left a note for the principal as to the exact assignments the child had to complete before he left.

4. *The teacher did not approach the child until the follow-through plan was completely prepared:* She did not meet with the child until she had completed her "homework"—that is, until she had done all she could to maximize the potential success of her follow-through efforts on behalf of the child.

PUTTING FOLLOW-THROUGH INTO ACTION: ASSERTIVE CONFRONTATIONS

A confrontation is a test of "wills" and "power." No teacher enjoys a confrontation, for it produces stress and anxiety. All children with behavior problems confront the teacher's authority, day in and day out. They do this through their active or passive refusal to do what is asked of them, be it their work, following directions, staying in their seats, playing cooperatively, etc.

In a confrontation with a child who has been a behavior problem at school, a teacher needs to be able to assert herself, in a manner which will reestablish her rights and authority in relation to the child. In an *assertive confrontation*, the teacher sends the child the following message: "There is no way I am going to tolerate your disregard of my requests! You *can* behave—and I am going to do everything I can to get you to choose to behave!" The teacher does not have this confrontation with the child until she is thoroughly prepared. "Prepared" means she knows what she wants the child to do and she has planned the limit-setting, follow-through consequences.

Specifically, in an assertive confrontation, the teacher sits down with the child and clearly and firmly tells the child: (1) the behavior expected from the child (assertive demand); (2) what will be done if the child does not choose to respond to the demands; and (3) why this is being done. The confrontation should be held when no other children are present, so as not to embarrass the child. If appropriate, the principal, the parents, and/or other teachers should be present to reinforce the teacher's demands. Here is an example of a typical assertive confrontation:

Teacher: "Mike, I want to talk to you. Please sit down."

Mike: "Why? I didn't do anything."

Teacher (looking Mike in the eye, firm tone of voice): "Mike, you can no longer disrupt the class; you will do your work when I tell you to." (Assertive Demand)

Mike: "You always pick on me. I do my work."

Teacher: "Mike, you will do your work when I tell you to." (Broken Record)

Mike: "Alright, I know you mean it."

Teacher: "Yes, Mike, and if you choose to disrupt and not do your work your parents will be called."

Mike: "My parents don't care what you say."

Teacher: "Yes they do, Mike. I spoke to your mom ten minutes ago and she and your dad will not tolerate your disruptiveness, either. If you disrupt, you will lose TV for the night." (demonstrates limit-setting, follow-through)

Mike: "You just want to get me into trouble. You don't like me."

Teacher: "Mike, I care too much about you to allow you to disrupt the class and not do your work. For you to enjoy school, you need to behave and do your work. Mike, I also care too much about myself to let you, or any other child, disrupt my class the way you do and get away with it." (Reasons for Doing It)

Mike: "It's hard for me to do the work."

Teacher: "I understand, Mike. I'll be there to help if you need it, simply raise your hand. Now, Mike, I want to be sure you understand what I have said. Tell me what you heard."

Mike: "If I disrupt and do not work, you will call my parents. If I need help I'm to raise my hand. Do you mean if I don't do one assignment, you will call my parents?"

Teacher: "That's correct. There is no reason why you cannot do all of the work like the rest of your classmates!"

POSITIVE
ASSERTIONS

VERBAL AND
FOLLOW-THROUGH

What do you do when the children act as you want them to? Unfortunately, most teachers would respond with an answer of "usually nothing." In other words, they would respond non-assertively; they would do nothing to influence the continuation of the behavior that they want and need from the children.

Why is this so? Truthfully, we think most teachers are so involved in dealing with behavior problems that they just don't have the time or energy to respond to those children who are acting appropriately. We feel teachers assume this pattern of behavior in the classroom because of several basic misconceptions. Many teachers have been taught that the only way they can get what they want in the classroom (e.g., quiet, independent work, cooperation) is to "get on" those children who act inappropriately. One 3rd grade teacher told us: "I'd love to have the opportunity to spend more time with the children when they are good, but I have so many behavior problems that I am occupied from the beginning of class until the final bell. If I didn't deal with those kids when they were bad, I would have chaos." Other teachers still hold to the belief that children are "just supposed to be good." As a result, they feel their energies need to be directed towards interacting with the children when they are "bad," not when they are "good."

We need to come right to the point of this section. It will be well worth it—to you and your students—for you to balance the amount of time and energy you utilize responding to the children's positive as well as problem behavior. Let's look at the benefits for you and your students when you respond consistently in an assertive manner to their appropriate behavior.

You will maximize your influence with regard to the

children's behavior. When you assertively recognize appropriate behavior, you will provide the children a positive consequence for their actions. The children will learn that the consequences for their appropriate behavior are responses that meet their wants and needs. Thus, the children are more likely to continue their appropriate behavior in order to receive the responses they like. Through combining your positive consequences for appropriate behavior and negative consequences for problem behavior, you can clearly establish the parameters of the behavior you want and don't want. You will be in the position to motivate the children to make the choice to eliminate their problem behavior and increase their appropriate behavior.

You can reduce the frequency of problem behavior. All children want your attention! If they feel they can't get it by being "good," then they will try to get it by being "bad." If you recognize and respond only to their negative behavior, the children will continue to act up in order to receive the attention from you that they can. By responding assertively to the positive behavior, you can quickly teach the children that they can get the attention they want and need by acting appropriately, rather than inappropriately. When the children learn this, they can and will choose to act in a positive rather than negative manner. An 8th grade student summed it up well when he told us: "The only time my English teacher would talk to me was when he was getting on me for 'messing up.' You know, something has happened to him. He's changed. Now he's nice to me when I'm doing my work. He talks to me and really lets me know he likes what I'm doing. I have been doing better, and he actually sent a note home to my folks telling them so. You know,

I still don't dig English, but I like it more, and I don't feel like 'goofin' around like I used to." The use of positive, assertive responses, thus, can reduce the frequency of problem behavior and reduce the time and energy you will need to put into responding to classroom disruptions.

You will create a more positive classroom environment which is easier to work in. The classroom is a "hassle" for you and the children if you feel the only way you can make the children behave is to be on their backs. It's hard work and creates tension between you and the children. The more you utilize praise and support to influence behavior, the better the children will feel about you and you will feel about yourself. As a 4th grade teacher told me, "Since I have been consistently more positive with my kids, they just don't fight me anymore. The more I praise the kids, the less I have to discipline them. It is so much nicer for both the kids and me. We still have our days, but nothing like the ones we used to have when I was constantly on them."

Again, planning is necessary for any teacher to develop a persistently positive, assertive response style. You will need to back-track and, again, quickly review what behavior you want from your students. Your planning, then, needs to progress as to how you will respond when the children do what you want.

In order for your positive responses to be meaningful, they need to be:

1. Responses you are comfortable with (i.e., you may be comfortable praising a child, but not giving him candy for appropriate behavior).

2. Something the *child* wants and enjoys.

3. Provided as soon as possible after the child chooses to behave appropriately (i.e., if you see the child working, *immediately* tell him you like it).

4. Provided as often as possible.

5. Planned out before being utilized.

When planning your positive responses you will first need to determine how you will respond verbally to the children's positive behavior. Your comments ("fine work," "well done," "excellent effort," "far out," etc.) and statements ("I like the work you did," "I like how well you stayed in your seat," "I like how you were quiet during work time") are the easiest vehicles you have to demonstrate assertively to the children your recognition and support of their appropriate behavior. As with verbal limit-setting, how you deliver your positive message is as important as what you say. Therefore, the same basic assertive communication exercise you performed with regard to limit-setting will be useful in perfecting this approach. With a partner, do the following:

Sit or stand, looking at one another. You begin by sending message, "I like the way you are working." Then reverse roles, and you receive the same message from your partner. Then, go through the rest of these steps:

1. Say, "I like the way you are working," while looking over your partner's shoulder. Be sure not to make eye contact.

2. Say, "I like the way you are working," looking your partner right in the eye.

3. Include your partner's first name before you deliver the praise, "Susan, I like the way you are working."

4. When delivering the message, utilize eye contact, first name, and, in addition, touch your partner in a manner which will communicate your approval (i.e., put your hand on her shoulder).

5. Repeat #1, looking over your shoulder.

6. Repeat #5, using eye contact, name, and touch.

When performing this exercise, you should experience again the significance of how you deliver your message. Eye contact, name, and touch can increase the impact of your positive communications, as well as your limit-setting demands. Remember, determine how most effectively you can deliver your message. Don't touch the students who do not like being touched, etc.

One important point with relation to positive, verbal assertions. Some students, especially adolescents, can be embarrassed if they are singled out in front of their peers for excessive praise. These students may become uncomfortable and begin disrupting in order not to be looked upon as a "goody goody" or the "Teacher's Pet." With some students, you will be most effective if you assert yourself positively when you are alone with them in class, after class, or during recess.

Hand in hand with verbal responses go non-verbal responses. A hug can say as much as, or more than, a countless "I like that." A smile, a wink, a pat on the shoulder, all can communicate clearly your positive support to the child.

On the other hand, some children will not be motivated sufficiently by your verbal assertions. Some children simply don't care if they do or do not please you. Some children are very uncomfortable with praise. And, some may need more motivation from you than just a "good job." With these children you will need to support your words with appropriate, positive consequences. You will need to utilize *Positive Follow-Through.*

When you utilize positive follow-through, you are providing the student an appropriate consequence for his appropriate behavior. The consequences are designed to help the student to increase his appropriate behavior. For example, you may tell a child: "If you complete your work, then you can play with a puzzle"; or, "If you do not shout out today, then I will spend some time reading you your favorite story"; or, "If you do all your work this week, then I will send home a positive note to your parents"; or, "If you do all your homework assignments, Monday through Wednesday, then you will not have homework on Thursday."

The first aspect of planning follow-through is to determine what the follow-through consequences will be. The consequence has to be something that the child wants and you are comfortable in providing. With the majority of children it is easy to determine the consequence if you know what they like and want. If a child always begs to be monitor, you know that being monitor would probably be an excellent consequence for him; or, if a child loves free time, this consequence would work for that particular child. If you have any trouble determining what consequences would work for a child, utilize the *Positive Assertive Follow-Through Survey* (p. 186).

Here are some follow-through consequences that we have seen utilized successfully by various teachers:

You. You, in many instances, are the *best* follow-through consequence the child can receive. Providing the child an opportunity to receive special attention from you can prove to be of great positive significance, especially at the elementary level where your importance to the children cannot be overemphasized. Many children would do just about anything to be able to spend time alone with the teacher, work together on a special project, or just stay after school to help out. One teacher we know used to take the children to McDonald's for a coke as a "reward" for their demonstrating significant improvement in their academic or social behavior. For most of the children, this short trip was a highlight of their school year.

Positive Notes or Phone Calls to Parents. A positive note or a phone call home to the child's parents can be a great boost for the child, and his parents as well. It can indicate the teacher's clear recognition and support of the child's appropriate behavior. For some children such positive attention from a teacher can be a new experience. It can prove to be a meaningful boost to their feelings about school, you, and their self-image.

Awards. Special awards for good behavior, good academic work, etc., can be highly significant motivators for many children. You can design your own awards or copy designs from other teachers. If your principal is cooperative, it is useful to have him give out special *Principal Awards* to students in recognition of their appropriate behavior.

Special Privileges. As a consequence for his appropriate behavior, the teacher allows the child the privilege of engaging in an activity that the child enjoys. Here are some suggestions:

P.E.

games

puzzles

choosing group activity

tutoring younger children

helping the teacher

first in line

choose friend to do an
   activity with

special projects

take care of class pet

monitor jobs

bring toy from home

read special book

cooking

typing

tape record voice

teach class an assignment

lead a discussion

assist the principal

work on hobby

building blocks

correct papers

Material Consequences. The child can be given material consequences for his appropriate behavior. Suggestions:

raisins

peanuts

sunflower seeds

cookies

fruit

ice cream

extra lunch from "free
   lunch" program

McDonald's hamburger

small pets

pencil

arts and crafts supplies

comic books

toy car—"Hot Wheels"

models

coloring books

marbles

toy jewelry

books

dolls

Home Follow-Through. With the cooperation of the parents, the child will receive a special privilege, material consequence, etc., at home for his appropriate behavior at school (i.e., "If you complete all your work you will get to watch an extra half hour of TV"). Home follow-through requires careful planning and preparation, the same as a limit-setting, home follow-through consequence would.

Contracts.

One of the most useful methods of planning and structuring the implementation of follow-through consequences is to use a *contract.* Basically, all that a contract is, is an agreement between the teacher and the child: "If you do this, in return, I will do this."

"If you will complete ten math problems, in return, I will allow you five extra minutes of free choice."

"If you will go one hour without fighting, in return, I will give you a piece of candy."

"If you go 30 minutes only speaking when called on, in return, I will give you a point on your card. When you get five points you will receive a gift from our grab bag."

A Contract, to be Useful, Needs to be:

1. *Positive in design.* "If you finish your reading, in return, I will give you extra free time," rather than, "If you don't finish, in return, I will give you an 'F.' "

2. *Designed to deliver any positive consequence quickly.* Many contracts require that the child will receive points or other symbolic reinforcers for certain amounts of appropriate behavior: "For every hour you keep your hands to yourself, you will receive one point. When you receive five points, you will get a special art project." As a general rule, the

younger the child, the more quickly he needs his positive consequence.

Kindergarten through third grade—every day

Fourth through fifth grade—every day to every three days

Sixth grade—every day to five days

Seventh grade and up—every day to three weeks.

3. *Flexible.* Initially, try the contract for a one-week period to see if it is effective. If within that week it is obvious that it is not working, be prepared to change it. It may be that the consequences the child is receiving are not what he wants, or he may have to wait too long before he receives them. If the contract is not working, rewrite it as needed.

4. *Designed to include limit-setting consequences.* Be sure to include the limit-setting consequences. You will end up with the contract that will say: "For every assignment you complete, you will earn three minutes with me to work on a special project. But, whenever you shout out, you will be timed out for ten minutes."

We want to illustrate further the planning and preparation that go into a follow-through effort, especially one that includes a contract. We will do this by discussing, step by step, the efforts of a 4th grade teacher, Mr. S., and a child in his class, James.

James was from a deprived background; he lived with his mother and three brothers and sisters. He was a poorly motivated child, with average academic abilities. He spent what seemed like the majority of his time disrupting his classmates, making "silly" comments, and getting out of his seat. The only time he was truly productive was during arts and crafts. He loved it, and was very creative. Mr. S. had been assertive with James and had set firm limits on his disruptive behavior. James was timed out in a neighboring teacher's room whenever he was disruptive. This had helped to eliminate a great deal of his disruptive behavior, but James still rarely completed any of his assignments. Mr. S. had been verbally assertive when James was working or completed an assignment. James seemed to like the praise, but it obviously did not influence him to the degree his teacher wanted it to. Mr. S. thus planned and utilized the following assertive follow-through plan with James.

1. He determined the behavior he would use assertively as a follow-through, which was getting James to complete his assignments.

2. He carefully thought about what consequences he had available that would motivate James to increase the number of completed assignments. Extra arts and crafts time seemed the obvious consequence for a child who had such a love for the particular activity.

3. He consulted with James to make sure that extra arts and crafts time would be something that he would like to earn more time doing. James' excited response indicated that Mr. S. was correct.

4. He prepared special arts and crafts projects for James to work on during his extra free time. He made sure

they were projects that James could do in a limited period of time and which would not require James to spend all of his time getting the supplies ready and then having to clean up the supplies.

5. He planned a contract to help him structure the follow-through. He spent some time determining how many minutes of extra arts and crafts time James could earn for completing each assignment. There were four assignments each day. He decided to try out five minutes per completed assignment. James could thus earn up to 20 minutes per day. In order that they could keep track of the time James earned, Mr. S. got a 3"×5" card to tape to James' desk. Whenever James completed an assignment, Mr. S. planned to give him a check, each being worth five minutes of time. He also determined that it would be easiest for James to have his arts and crafts time at the end of the day, right before the children went home.

6. He met again with James when he had worked out all the details. He explained the contract to James and, again, reminded James about the fact that if he disrupted he would choose to be timed out in the classroom next door. Together they wrote a copy of the contract and they both signed it. James was overwhelmed with the prospect of earning extra arts and crafts time and couldn't wait to begin the contract.

7. James did extremely well the first two weeks. Each day he earned between 15 and 20 minutes and did not choose to be timed out once. Along with the contract, Mr. S. continued to be persistent and recognize James' appropriate behavior verbally.

By the third week it became clear that James was tiring

of the extra arts and crafts time. Mr. S. met with him again, and together they came up with a new follow-through consequence. James could earn time reading alone with the teacher. Because of the time limitation, James would earn only two minutes for each assignment he completed. James did not mind; he was excited again at the prospect of all that attention from his teacher.

By the fourth week James was consistently completing all of his work. Mr. S. felt James was doing much better and would still be motivated to do his work with less time for each completed assignment. Mr. S. reduced the time to one minute per assignment.

James maintained his excellent behavior and by the sixth week Mr. S. eliminated the time with James completely. He was careful, though, to remember to praise James persistently when he demonstrated good work habits.

Mr. S.'s concern and planning helped James to turn around a cycle of failure. James' academic achievement naturally improved because of the extra effort he was motivated to put forth in his classroom assignments.

This teacher's efforts encompassed all of the key principles of assertive follow-through:

1. He did not assume the behavior of others (i.e., the child);

2. He anticipated possible problems that might occur;

3. He left nothing to doubt; and

4. He did not meet with the child until he was completely prepared. The use of the principles enabled the teacher to assert himself successfully with a difficult child.

There are three questions that typically are raised by teachers in regard to positive follow-through: (1) Isn't it bribery? (2) How long do I have to utilize the follow-through consequence? (3) What will the other children say or do?

Isn't it bribery? Positive follow-through consequences can become bribery if the teacher allows them to. When the teacher approaches the children in a non-assertive manner which communicates, "Kids, I'm desperate, I'll even pay you off with M&M's, whatever, as long as you are good," bribery or worse occurs. The teacher may at first try to bribe the children to be "good," but in the end the children will end up extorting the M&M's from the teacher in payment for their not disrupting. We remember watching a desperate, non-assertive teacher who discovered the magic of giving the children candy when they were good. She relied on the candy, *not herself*, to control the children's behavior. The children knew this and continually demanded more and more candy for the same "good" behavior. If she had taken the candy away, we feel that chaos would have resulted.

The teacher, not the candy, etc., has to influence the child's behavior. The candy is only a tool the teacher chooses to utilize in order to get her needs met. The teacher has to communicate clearly to the children the following message, "I will provide you candy, etc., because I feel it will *help me* to influence you to improve your behavior. If it doesn't work out, or you try to abuse the special reward, I will eliminate it!"

How long do I need to utilize the follow-through consequences? As long as you feel you need to in order to get your needs met and help the child. One word of advice, don't eliminate the consequences all at once. Gradually fade them out, such as Mr. S. did in the vignette. He reduced the time James earned from two minutes per completed assignment, to one minute. Gradually fading out the consequences will help you to maintain a more consistent influence with regards to the children's behavior.

What will the other children say or do? It seems as though most teachers have the fear that if they single out one or two children for special attention, the rest of the children will either have a "jealous fit," or all begin to disrupt so that they, too, can get the same attention. Let's look at what really happens.

To start with, the children are well aware of those students who have special problems in their class. It is no secret that one child constantly yells and screams, or that another has daily tantrums, etc. The disruptions of those children bother the other children, just as they bother you. The children want their peers to behave just as you do. The children, thus, are usually glad when the teacher puts in the extra effort to "help" a child to improve his disruptive behavior. The children, as well, become aware that the teacher is someone who cares about children with problems and tries to help them. This can reassure them, for they will realize that if they have a problem there will be someone there to help them, too.

The only time a teacher will have problems in singling out certain children for extra attention is when they are not meeting the other children's needs for positive support and attention. If a teacher is basically non-assertive when the children act appropriately, and suddenly showers a student with praise and special privileges, the other children will become jealous and act up. If you are consistently assertive with the other children, their basic needs will be met and they will have no need to become jealous or act up.

Before we finish this section, we want to emphasize that we're not stating that you should use positive assertions instead of limit-setting assertions. What is needed is a *balance* between the two. As we have discussed, it's to your benefit to utilize positive assertions whenever possible to influence the children's behavior. Positive assertions, though, should not be utilized to the exclusion of limit-setting responses. There are, of course, times the children need your limits. On the other hand, don't utilize limit-setting responses to the exclusion of positive assertions. *Strive for a balance!*

8

BUT, WHAT IF THEY ALL DO IT?

ASSERTIVE CLASSROOM MANAGEMENT SKILLS

Assertive classroom management does not begin the first day of school: It starts with the planning of your discipline efforts in the days before school starts! Just as you plan how to reach your academic objectives with your students, you need to plan how you will reach your behavioral objectives.

Within the area of classroom management planning, initial efforts need to include how you will assert yourself the first day and week of school. Therefore, effective planning will include these components:

1. Behaviors you want the first day/week of school.

2. Limit-setting consequences you will employ the first day/week.

3. Positive consequences you will employ the first day/week.

Your planning should follow the principles discussed in the previous chapters. One point will be obviously different. When determining positive and limit-setting follow-through consequences, you will want to determine those consequences which will influence the majority of your class, not just selected students.

On the first day of school, you will want to communicate your wants verbally to your students and demonstrate that you are prepared to back up your words with appropriate consequences. In addition to your verbal communications, it is useful to do one or all of the following: (1) make a chart for your room which covers the behavior you want; (2) have the students (if appropriate) write down the behavior you want, and keep it on their desks; (3) have the students write a letter to their parents which covers your discipline guidelines. Have the parents read, sign, and return the letter. Here is an example of how a teacher may assertively present her discipline guidelines to her students on the first day.

"I am looking forward to a good year with all of you. As your teacher, there are behaviors I need and want from you, so that I can do the best possible job in this classroom. Here is what I want and need from each and every one of you: (teacher writes the requests on the board).

1. Follow my directions the first time I give them.

2. Stay in your seat unless you have permission to get up.

3. Raise your hand and wait to be called upon before you speak, during discussions or work time.

4. Keep your hands, feet, and objects to yourself.

5. No cussing or teasing.

Now, I want to be sure you understand what I want. So, I want each of you to take out a clean piece of paper and write down these rules. I will want each of you to take this sheet home and have your parents read, sign, and return it to me.

Now, I will not tolerate any student not following my rules. I have a responsibility to all of you, and myself, to make sure this is a classroom where we can all work free from disruptions. If any student chooses to disregard the rules, I will do the following: (teacher writes on the board).

1. The first time you do not follow directions, shout out, or bother someone, I will put your name on the board.

When your name goes on the board, it means you will have to stay after school that day for ten minutes.

2. If you again choose to disrupt, I will put a check next to your name. One check equals an additional ten minutes after school.

3. If you get your name and more than two checks on the board during the day, I will call your parents.

I also have a responsibility to all of you to let you know that I like it when you do what I want, and when you contribute to a positive classroom environment. Thus, I have here an empty jar, and a bag of marbles. Each marble that goes in the jar will earn the entire class 30 seconds of free choice, to be collected at the end of each day. The more you follow the class rules, the more marbles you will earn. Do you have any questions as to the behavior I want? What will I do if you do not do what I want? What will I do if you do what I want?" (Both limit-setting and positive guidelines for the class will be included in the students' letter to their parents.)

The first few days of school, most students are on their best behavior. This affords you with an excellent opportunity to establish a positive rapport with your class. The more positive you are when you first work with the students, the less you will need to set limits. This point is particularly valid with potential behavior problems. Be sure to provide such students the maximum positive attention you possibly can, in order to help them establish positive behavior patterns in your class.

One way we recommend for establishing such positive rapport with your students is to do the following. The first two weeks (four weeks on a secondary level) call or send home a note to each parent, reporting on a positive aspect of their child's first few days at school. This immediately lets each student and parent know you can be counted upon actively to recognize and support the student's positive behavior. The short time it takes to write a brief note, or make a brief call, is time very well spent.

A note or a call home also helps establish a positive, working relationship with the parents. Such a relationship can be crucial in dealing effectively with the behavior of certain students. To foster this relationship further, we always recommend sending home a letter to the parents during the first few days in which you assertively outline your philosophy relating to parents. Here is an example of such a letter:

Dear Parent,
   I would like to take this opportunity to share with you my approach to teaching. I feel it is vital and in the best interest of your child that there exist close home-school communication. I feel you have the right to know how your child is doing at school. In order to reach this goal, I feel it is my responsibility to keep you informed as to progress or lack of progress of your child. I will, thus, be sending home a note or calling you in the near future.
   I am looking forward to working with you in the coming year.

Sincerely,

Just as it is important to establish a positive working relationship with the parents, the same situation exists in relationship with your principal. Once you have prepared your discipline plans for the new semester, share them with your principal. Principals, in general, are impressed by teachers who have clearly defined objectives with regard to discipline. Also, such a meeting can provide you with the opportunity to discuss what support you will need from the principal in relation to your discipline efforts.

No matter how assertively you begin a school year, you will need to plan how you will deal with any classroom management problems that may occur. It is necessary to remember that emphasis in assertive classroom management is on conciseness, the ability to communicate your wants and needs in the most direct manner possible. To be concise requires that both positive and limit-setting follow-through efforts be planned in advance so that they can be utilized easily and effectively.

In the chapter on limit-setting follow-through, we discussed some basic limit-setting consequences which can be used as well with classroom management problems. Keeping groups of disruptive students after school, calling their parents, having them miss free-choice time, etc., can all be effective if you plan and persist in your efforts.

In relation to positive follow-through, we *always* employ a positive follow-through effort that involves all of the students. We do this for two reasons: (1) it enables us more effectively to motivate appropriate behavior, and (2) most of all, it is fun to do! Here are some examples of positive consequences that teachers have employed successfully (especially at the elementary level):

Marbles in a Jar. This is the consequence most frequently used by teachers we work with, because it is so simple and versatile. When the class is doing what you want, you take a marble and drop it in a jar. The sound of the marble dropping into the jar immediately lets the students know they are doing what you want and that you recognize their efforts. Each marble can be worth, for example, 30 seconds to one minute of free choice at the end of the day, one minute towards a party on Friday, etc. Or, the class can earn a party, movie, picnic, etc., when they have filled the entire jar.

When the class is particularly good, you can add "bonus" marbles in recognition of their behavior. Finally, you can single out an individual student's "super" or "improved" behavior for recognition with extra marbles.

Teachers at all grade levels report that the Marble in the Jar is an extremely effective means of motivating appropriate behavior, even with the most difficult class!

Secret Words. Determine a positive consequence for the class. For example, a popcorn party. When the students demonstrate appropriate behavior, put the first letter of the consequence on the board (i.e., "P"). When the class' behavior has enabled you to put all of the letters on the board—POPCORN PARTY—the class receives the surprise.

Grab Bag. In the "grab bag" have tickets that entitle a child to do one of the following: have a bag of peanuts; earn a pencil; be team leader for a day; be special monitor for a day; be the teacher's helper for the afternoon; receive extra free time. Children earn the right to go to the "grab bag" for special positive behavior, or noticeable improvement in their behavior.

Rent Classroom "Valuables." Through their appropriate behavior, children can earn the right to "rent" for a specified period of time (i.e., overnight, weekend, etc.) "valuables" from the classroom. For example, you may want to use classroom pets, puzzles, games, special books, or toys.

White Elephant Raffle. The children bring in a "white elephant" from home—toys, jewelry, etc. The major premise for this consequence is: "One man's junk is another man's treasure." The children earn raffle tickets through their appropriate behavior. At the end of the week have the raffle.

Employ each of these consequences until their novelty wears off. Then be prepared to employ a different one. For some classes, though, the novelty may not wear off until the end of the year.

To provide further assistance in dealing with classroom management problems, we would like to conclude this chapter with some examples of how other teachers have handled such problems assertively.

Ms. L. had the noisiest 3rd grade class of her short teaching career. It seemed as though they were constantly shouting out throughout the entire day. Ms. L. tried to praise those who did not shout out, but that had no effect. Finally, Ms. L. decided to handle the situation assertively. On Monday morning she called a class meeting and assertively confronted the class. She placed her demand, "Stop shouting out"; presented her follow-through consequences, "Whoever shouts out will have their parents called that night"; and told them her reason for doing so, "I will not tolerate children disrupting each other—and me—period!" The first day eight children shouted out. That night *all* of their parents were called. The parents were told what their child had done and asked to follow through at home with a consequence. The next day four children shouted out and their parents were called. The following day only two acted inappropriately, and then zero. Ms. L. let those who were quiet clearly know how much she appreciated their cooperation. After a rough week, it was obvious that

Ms. L.'s assertive responses had definitely helped to eliminate a potentially chaotic, unproductive problem.

Ms. P.'s 6th grade class consisted of a number of hostile
children who would constantly provoke each other and
the other classmates. This resulted in a constant chorus
of "stop hitting me" and "teacher, he's bothering me."
Ms. P. demanded that the children "stop disrupting"; and
to follow-through, she made a contract with the class,
which went as follows: "For each hour that you can function without hitting or pushing one another, the whole
class will earn one point. When you have 25 points, you
will get to see a Walt Disney movie. If, however, anyone
hits or pushes, the class will lose one point; and the person involved will have to do his work in the corner for
one half hour." The contract worked immediately, for
the children wanted to see the movie and didn't like to
be timed out. Ms. P. observed that not only did the children quickly settle down, they also attempted to control
the "troublemakers" by telling them to "cool it." It was
necessary to time out several children, but the situation
improved dramatically within a short period of time.

Sam was one of the most difficult 5th grade boys Ms. S.
had ever taught. He was the classic "class clown" and,
as a result, was very disruptive. When he did "his own
thing" the children would go wild and give him all the
attention he needed. His energies were so inappropriately
directed that he accomplished very little work, and became further and further behind in his assignments. Ms.
S. met alone with Sam and presented her demands. She
also held a class meeting and presented her demands to
the class. These demands for the entire class were: "Stop
responding to Sam's disruptions. For each hour you ignore
him, the class will earn two minutes of free time. Anyone who laughs at Sam or takes part in his disruptions

will be timed out. I will not tolerate children not doing their work and making themselves the brunt of their classmates' laughter." Ms. S.' assertiveness with Sam and the class paid off. Sam began to control his behavior; and when he did not, he did not have an "audience" to keep his performance going.

THE ASSERTIVE DISCIPLINE PLAN AND OTHER PERSISTENCY BUILDING PROCEDURES

Throughout the previous chapters, we have stressed the need for you to respond persistently in an assertive manner in order to maximize the potential influence of your efforts. In the stress and strain of today's classroom, this is easier said than done! You will not develop a persistently assertive response style overnight—it will obviously take time and practice. Being aware of this, we have developed or incorporated various procedures which can help you rapidly increase your ability to persistently respond assertively.

Assertive Discipline Plan

The Assertive Discipline Plan should serve as the foundation of your discipline efforts. In the preceding chapters we have discussed planning and its value in any assertive effort. At this point we need to elaborate upon our previous comments.

Planning is essential to good teaching. It is an accepted fact that it takes careful planning in order to teach academic material. Few teachers enter their classrooms without some form of lesson plan to structure and guide their efforts. And, when lessons do not reach their predetermined objectives, most teachers will systematically analyze the lesson, modifying and changing the lesson to increase its effectiveness.

Lesson planning is basically second nature to teachers. As a teacher, you have been exposed to the principles ever since you first enrolled in education classes. Lesson plans are part of your professional routine, and you do them almost automatically when the need arises. However, planning for discipline efforts is an entirely different story.

The vast majority of teachers have never learned nor been exposed to the steps involved in planning discipline programs, especially those to be used specifically with disruptive students. This is exceedingly apparent whenever we observe teachers discussing their problem students with one another. Because of the teachers' frustrations, all we often hear is their complaining about how difficult the students are.

Teacher A: "Mark is one of the roughest kids I've ever had!"

Teacher B: "I know. I had him last year."

Teacher A: "I don't know how much longer I can take that kid in my classroom. He drives me nuts. How did you handle him all year?"

Teacher B: "I don't know—it was rough. I hope I don't get any more like him!"

Such complaining may help (in a very small way) to relieve the strain of dealing with difficult students, but it in no way helps to solve the problem. What we are saying is this: planning your discipline efforts, and utilizing the previously described assertive principles, are as essential to your teaching as is your lesson planning. Discipline planning will structure and guide your classroom management efforts the same as lesson planning facilitates your academic efforts.

What does discipline planning entail? Basically, it is the systematic application of the assertive principles you have already learned. It involves periodically at the end of the day, week, etc., focusing your attention on any *ex-*

isting or *potential* discipline problems you may have.
These discipline problems may involve an individual student, a group of students, or the entire class. With each
problem, utilize the following problem-solving planning:

1. What behavior(s) do I want the student(s) to eliminate?—or engage in?

2. What limit-setting consequences will be appropriate?

3. What positive consequences will be appropriate?

4. What planning is necessary to implement the limit-
   setting and/or positive consequences?

Here is a good example of what we mean:

Ms. T. had difficulty in dealing with Jamie, a 3rd grader.
When the class sat on the rug for stories or discussions,
Jamie would frequently poke the other children, shout
out the answers, or get up and wander around the room.
Ms. T. had talked to Jamie about his problem behavior
and praised him when he was good, but nothing worked.
Finally, she sat down and read through the guidelines of
discipline planning.
   First, she determined the behaviors she wanted Jamie
to eliminate: poking, shouting out, getting up. Then she
determined the behaviors that she wanted: keep hands to
himself, raise hand and wait to be called on, sit on rug.
   Next, she determined the limit-setting consequences.
Jamie did not like to be isolated from the group, so she
decided to send him to the corner for ten minutes whenever he engaged in disruptive behavior.

For positive consequences, she felt that Jamie would like to have positive notes sent home to his parents. Therefore, he could earn a note sent home if he did not disrupt for the entire day.

Finally, Ms. T. focused on what planning was needed to implement the limit-setting and positive consequences. She decided it was necessary to discuss with the parents what she was going to do, so that they would be prepared to follow-through at home. Also, Ms. T. Made copies of the positive note that she would send home, so they would be ready when Jamie earned them. Her last step was to meet with Jamie.

It can be clearly seen that the teacher in the previous example, through her discipline planning, was well prepared to deal assertively with her student. She knew what she wanted, and how to maximize her potential influence in order to get her needs met. With more difficult situations, it may be useful to engage in problem solving and discipline planning with our peers, school psychologist, principal, or anyone who may be familiar with your students and/or who has successfully managed similar problems. Note the following example.

Wes was the class clown. He took great pleasure in being the center of attention in his 6th grade classroom. During work time he would make loud animal noises, tell jokes, and draw provocative pictures which he would hold up for all to see. His teacher, Mr. L., had never encountered a student such as Wes. He knew what behavior he wanted Wes to eliminate (the noises, jokes, and drawings), and what behavior he wanted Wes to engage in (do his work); but, he was not sure as to what consequences would be the most effective in influencing Wes' behavior. He decided to meet with Ms. Y., Wes' 5th grade teacher, as she had been quite successful in dealing with Wes the previous year.

In the meeting, Mr. L. learned which limit-setting and positive consequences had been effective with Wes. The best limit-setting consequence was to send Wes to another classroom and have him do his work alone in the corner. The most successful positive consequence was allowing him to earn the opportunity to perform magic tricks, or tell jokes or riddles in front of the class.

Mr. L. decided to utilize the consequences suggested by Ms. Y. In deciding how to implement the program, he arranged with Ms. Y. to have Wes work in her room when he was disruptive in his own. No planning was needed for implementing the positive consequences, for Wes had more jokes and magic tricks than he would ever be able to share.

Discipline Planning is needed in one final area: Special Activities. By special activities, we mean those activities the students do not consistently engage in (e.g., field trips, assemblies). A day or so before such an activity, especially if there have been problems with such an activity in the past, engage in some basic discipline planning. Once again, determine the behaviors you do and do not want, the limit-setting and positive consequences, and how the program will be implemented. Here is an example of what we mean.

The teacher was to take his class to a school assembly. Through his planning, he determined the behaviors he did not want: talking during the performance, booing, hitting. Behaviors he did want: sitting quietly. The limit-setting consequences: stay after school and write 50 times

"I will not talk during assemblies," etc. Positive consequence: praise. Implementation: be sure to tell the students before the assembly what he wanted and what the consequences would be.

The following are additional procedures which will prove useful in assisting you in developing a persistently assertive response style.

Mental Rehearsal. The more you visualize a specific situation and think about how you will respond assertively to it, the higher is the probability that you will respond automatically in an assertive manner when the situation occurs. Mental Rehearsal is designed to be used on a daily basis to help you increase your consistency in recognizing and responding assertively to difficult situations. The process requires you to visualize and think about specific situations and how you would want to respond assertively. By using this approach, when the situation does occur in your classroom, you will be mentally prepared to act appropriately. Note this example.

A teacher we worked with had difficulty dealing with a child who constantly got out of his seat. All too often, she would see him get out of his seat; but, for whatever reasons, she would get distracted and fail to respond assertively. In order to increase her consistency, each morning on her way to work she would mentally rehearse the picture of the child getting out of his seat and how she would respond assertively to him by timing him out in the corner. Thus, because of her rehearsals, when the child did get out of his seat, she responded almost automatically, as she had visualized, and timed him out in the corner. After a week, the child received the message and remained in his seat. If necessary, she could have utilized

the same process to increase her positive responses when
he stayed in his seat.

Write It Down. Leave as little to your memory as possible. The reason is simple: None of our memories are
perfect, and we all forget things! And, in the stimulation
and stress of teaching, it is very easy to forget things.

What you need to do is keep a piece of paper handy on
which you can record important reminders in relation
to follow-through: A child loses free time, jot down a
note to that effect; a child has had an especially good
morning, make a note to send a positive note home; a
child's behavior problems become more severe, keep
track of the number of occurrences and note to plan a
meeting with his parents.

During the day, periodically check your pad to be sure
that you are following through on your consequences,
and to remind yourself of things you still need to do.

You may want to write down additional reminders to
yourself, such as: Positive behaviors to look for (John in
his seat, Sue raising her hand); or, inappropriate behaviors (Sam out of his seat, Gary refusing to clean up).

Positive-Thought Actions. All too often, when a child is
behaving *appropriately,* the teacher does not consciously
recognize the behavior. Instead, the teacher may have a
quick flash of relief, or a brief thought such as "Thank
the Lord there are no hassles with him now." We are not
as conscious of such quick positive "flashes" or thoughts
as we are of the disturbing feelings and thoughts that
result when a child is disrupting. Thus, we do not respond
as frequently to positive behavior as we should. In order
to overcome this lack of consistency, you can train yourself to respond to the quick "flashes" and thoughts. When-

ever you have such a thought, *stop* for the split second it takes, and think "What is he doing that I like?" (i.e., is he working? in his seat? raising his hand?). Then act assertively on your positive thought by praising the child, "I like the way you are working." Through practice, the use of positive-thought actions will help you to increase the frequency and consistency of your positive assertions.

Positive Self-Assertions. Research demonstrates that one way for an individual to increase his confidence and consistency is to give himself positive self-feedback on his performance. In other words, if we like what we do and tell ourselves so, we will do a better job. Positive self-assertions are simply compliments we give ourselves for *our* "good" behavior (i.e., you do a consistent job of assertively complimenting a child, compliment yourself: "I did a good job with him this morning."). Now, you may feel this sounds corny.—"I'm not going to go around complimenting myself all day." Look at it this way. I'm sure you criticize yourself very freely when you "blow it" with a child. Self-criticism tears down your confidence; unless you build it up with positive self-feedback, you are making it more difficult on yourself to develop the confidence needed to be consistently assertive. All we can say is, try it—the results will be self-evident.

Relaxation Training. If you get so "uptight" in the classroom that it hinders your being consistently assertive, you should consider using Relaxation Training. This is a proven method which helps individuals relax under stressful situations, such as teaching. What you need to do is find a ten-minute period in which you can be alone; recess or lunch is perfect. Find a comfortable chair or, if available, a cot or couch. Get comfortable and do the following:

Settle back as comfortably as you can. Close your eyes
and alternately tense and relax the muscles in each part
of your body, beginning with the wrists and continuing
up the arms to the face, then back down the neck to the
shoulder, chest, stomach, pelvic region, lower back, thighs,
calves, and finally, feet. Tense and relax each of the parts
of your body twice. After you do each area, take a very
deep breath, hold it, and then exhale slowly. Notice how
you become further relaxed as you exhale. To increase
the effectiveness of the relaxation training, visualize in
your mind the muscles tensing and relaxing as you do it.

When you have progressed through the entire body, visualize clearly in your mind a very relaxing scene. Focus
on this scene, take five deep breaths, and allow your mind
and body to relax even further. When you feel ready, open
your eyes and get up slowly. You should feel relaxed, re-
freshed, and thus better able to deal with the stress and
strains that follow.

ASKING FOR HELP:

THE USE OF ASSERTIVE
SKILLS WITH PARENTS
AND PRINCIPALS

In a previous chapter we introduced the "Myth of a Good Teacher." Briefly restated, the "Myth" assumes a "good" teacher is one that is able to handle all of the problems with her students on her own and with no assistance from the principal, parents, or peers. This myth is obviously an influential force affecting a teacher's decision about how to manage a problem student, especially when she feels the need to ask for help with him.

As a direct result of this myth, teachers often seem to feel the only way they can approach the principal or parents for assistance is as a "beaten teacher." For example, the "beaten teacher" might say to the principal: "I give up. I'm at my wits' end with that child. I cannot take it any longer. Please, you have to do something to help me." Or, the "beaten teacher" might approach the parents with: "I've tried everything with your daughter. She's tearing my class apart, and I really don't know what to do with her. Something has to be done." Relating to others in such a helpless, overwhelmed manner only perpetuates the myth that there is something "wrong" with the teacher for needing assistance.

You have the right to ask the parents or principal for whatever assistance you deem necessary, in order to maximize your potential influence with a child! In this section we will discuss how to get this assistance from the child's parents and the principal.

ASKING THE PARENTS FOR HELP

Many teachers feel threatened and overwhelmed by parents, especially if the parents are pushy or manipulative. Thus, many teachers have difficulty in being assertive with parents; they do not clearly and firmly let the parents know what they want or need from them, nor do they stand up for their rights. As a result, all too often we hear teachers being woefully non-assertive. For example, when calling parents:

They apologize for bothering the parents: "I'm really sorry to bother you at home with this . . ."

They downgrade the problems: "We had a 'small' problem with your son today." (In reality, he had a violent tantrum which disrupted the entire class for 20 minutes.)

They belittle themselves: "I just don't know what to do with your son." (Yes, you do! You need the cooperation of the parents to discipline him at home for his tantrums.)

They do not clearly state their needs: "I know you are busy, working and all, but if you could find the time I'd appreciate it if you talked to your son about his tantrums." (You want her to discipline her son at home—period!)

They downgrade the consequences of the child's behavior. "I don't know what will happen if he doesn't change his behavior in class." (Yes, you do! He will need to be suspended.)

Often teachers confuse being assertive with being hostile. They are afraid that if they are assertive, the parent will be offended and go to the principal. However, hostility means that you express your wants and needs in a manner which offends others or violates their self-dignity. The difference between non-assertive, hostile, and assert-

ive communications with parents can best be illustrated
by a direct comparison of the different responses.

Situation: You call the parents in to discuss the behavior problems of their child. During the conference, the
parents become angry and unfairly blame you for their
child's problems at school.

Non-Assertive Response	*Hostile Response*	*Assertive Response*
You sit there and passively take the criticism without expressing your concerns and feelings.	You get defensive and tell the parents off, blaming them for their child's problems.	You listen to the criticism. You express your recognition of their feelings. *Again,* you express that you called them to arrange some constructive cooperation between you, which will help their child's behavior.

Situation: A child comes to school dirty and unkempt.
You call the parents to express your concern about the
child's cleanliness, and request that he come to school
better kempt. The parents balk at your request, as they
have in the past.

Non-Assertive Response	*Hostile Response*	*Assertive Response*
You listen to the parents and don't press your	You tell the parents that it is a disgrace the way	You firmly repeat your demand, and let the parents

| demands. | they send their child to school, and they should be ashamed of themselves | know that in the best interest of their child you will contact the appropriate agency, if the situation does not improve. |

Situation: You call the parents to ask their cooperation in following through at home on the contract you have with their child, as a result of the behavior problems he has in your class. The parents are very reluctant to do so.

| Non-Assertive Response | Hostile Response | Assertive Response |
| You give up and don't press your wants. | You tell the parents how inadequate they are, and that they had better learn to discipline their child. | You firmly repeat your demands, and let the parents know the consequences if their child continues to do poorly in school. |

As you have seen, in the assertive responses of each situation, the teacher stated her position and stuck to it. It was firm—not passive, not hostile. You, as a teacher, need to let the parents know where you stand and then allow them to *choose* whether to cooperate with your wishes. When you are non-assertive (passive), you allow the parents to "control you." You feel "lousy" and don't receive the support or action you need to help the child. When you are hostile, you "put down" the parents. They will become threatened and, again, you will not get what you want and need from them.

We have found that teachers can learn to be more assertive and, thus, more effective in their relations with parents. The model we utilize is simple, easily learned and implemented.

1. Assert yourself and contact the parents as soon as you see that there is, or possibly will be, a situation with the child where you will need the parents' cooperation.

2. Know what you want from your meeting or conversation with the parents. (Goal)

3. Plan how you will achieve the goal. (Objectives)

4. Know why you want the parents' cooperation and assistance. (Rationale)

5. Be prepared to explain what you feel will occur if the parents are not cooperative. (Consequences)

6. Have documentation to support your comments.

Assert Yourself Immediately. You can prevent many major problems by dealing with them when they are still small. As soon as you feel that there is a situation where you need the parents' involvement and support, call the parents and let them know what you will need from them. The first week is not too soon! This can: (1) lay the groundwork for future cooperation; (2) enable you to keep the parents fully informed of the child's progress, or lack of it; (3) prevent you from "surprising" the parents late in the year with a "crisis" call regarding a problem of which they were not aware.

Goals for Conference. Know specifically what you want from the parents, before they come in for a conference (i.e., "I need your cooperation in regard to your son's fighting at school"). Write the goal down before you meet with the parents.

Objectives for Conference. Determine, specifically, how you would like the parents to reach the goal (i.e., "I need you to provide some type of discipline when your son fights and I send a note home"). Work with the parents in determining how they can work most comfortably with you to achieve the goals (i.e., "How do you usually discipline your child? Do you feel that would be useful in this situation?").

Rationale for Conference. In the vast majority of conferences relating to children with behavior problems, the rationale is as follows: "I am meeting with you because it is in *your child's best interest* that we work together in helping him eliminate his problem behavior. You are the most important people in your child's life. You have more influence over him than I ever will. Your influence is vital to helping your child. Your child needs to know we are working together, and that we will do all we can to see that he chooses to improve his behavior."

Consequences that You Feel Will Occur if the Parents Do Not Cooperate. Be straight with the parents as to what you feel will happen if they do not support you. All too often, teachers are reluctant to "lay it on the line" with parents. This often results in the parents not realizing how serious the situation is with their child, and how vital their support is for improvement to occur (i.e., "If your son does not realize that you will not tolerate his fighting at school, it will make it much more difficult for us to work with him. He will continue to have trouble with his peer relationships. And, if his behavior [fighting] continues, we will be forced to suspend him."].

Documentation. It is useful to have complete documentation to support the assertions you make to the parents. When discussing their child's poor work habits, present several examples to the parents. If their child fights excessively, keep an anecdotal record of each incident, which you can show the parents.

ASSERTIVE COMMUNICATION SKILLS

We have incorporated a number of assertive techniques to assist you in your efforts *only* with parents who are uncooperative and/or manipulative. These techniques are useful in helping you to assert your wants when your normal approaches are not successful with the parents. One of the techniques you are familiar with: Broken Record. Two are new: Active Sending and Receiving of Messages, and Yes or No Response.

Broken Record:

This technique again is designed to help you make your point and stick to it. To utilize this technique you need to determine what you want from your interaction with the parents. In most conferences, it will be the "goal" you hope to achieve for the conference. This should be, as noted, in the form of a statement: "I need your cooperation in regard to your son's fighting at school." In your interaction with the parents, the "Broken Record" is evidenced by the repeated expression of the message, thereby disregarding the "side-tracking" responses of the parents.

Teacher: "I need your cooperation in regard to your son's fighting at school. (assertive statement)

Parent: "I know I need to discipline him at home when you send a note to me, but I'm so busy with all the other children. Do you know what I mean?"

Teacher: "I understand you are busy, but I still need your cooperation in regard to your son's fighting." (Broken Record)

Parent: "But it really hurts me to have to discipline him all the time. He gets so upset."

Teacher: "I understand it's hard, but I still need your cooperation in regard to your son's fighting." (Broken Record)

Parent: "You sure are persistent."

Teacher: "You're right. I feel your son needs to know clearly where you stand in terms of his fighting at school."

Parent: "I see your point. When I get a note that says he has had a fight, he will have no T.V. that night."

The "Broken Record" is also useful when the parents are more concerned with blaming you for their child's problems, rather than developing some solutions. When dealing with such parents, be sure to: (1) remain calm; (2) don't get defensive; and (3) don't get angry. Note the following example.

Teacher: "Mr. T., I need your cooperation with regard to helping your child do his reading."

Parent: "Ms. C., my child never had problems in the past. I think your teaching style is the problem."

Teacher (calmly): "I understand, but the point is your child is a grade behind in reading. I need your cooperation in helping your child with his reading." (Broken Record)

Parent: "But he never had problems until he came to your class."

Teacher (calmly): "I understand, but he has problems now. I need your cooperation in order to help your child." (Broken Record)

Parent: "Have you spoken to his previous teacher to see what she did differently?"

Teacher (calmly): "Yes, I have. The point is, however, that your child has a reading problem, and I need your cooperation in helping him with it." (Broken Record)

Parent: "Well, I don't understand what I can do to help."

Active Sending and Receiving of Messages

All too often, what you say to the parents is not what they hear—and vice versa. This can result in additional confusion and difficulties, as you must surely know from past experience. You can never be assured that the message you send will be received exactly as you intended, but you can maximize the potential by using active sending and receiving. The basic assumption of this technique is that one should not assume the transmission of an important message as accurately received—you need to check it out.

When receiving an important message from the parents, repeat the message to make sure that what you heard is what they meant to say.

Parent: "I'm going to talk with my husband about disciplining our son at home. He will come up with something."

Teacher: "Let me see if I understand you correctly. You and your husband will be discussing the discipline of your son at home. You will come up with a specific plan. Is that right?"

Parent: "That's correct."

Teacher: "Okay. You will get back to me as soon as you talk to your husband? At that point we will be ready to begin our efforts with your son. I want to make sure I was clear. What did you hear me saying?"

(Teacher is moving into *Active Sending* which involves asking the parent to repeat the message so that you know the parent clearly understands you.)

Parent: "I will get back to you as soon as I talk with my husband. Then we will begin our efforts with my son."

Teacher: "Sounds good to me."

Yes or No Response

Some parents will attempt to give "vague" responses when you request specific action from them (i.e., "Well, I'll think about what you said"; "What you said was interesting, I'll consider it"; or "I really want to do what you asked—I just don't know if it's possible"). All too often, these responses are simply attempts by the parents to get the teacher "off their backs." The statements, "I'll think about what you said," etc., may in reality mean "Don't bother me any more." If you do not pursue the issue, you will be left up in the air with no commitment, pro or con, from the parent. It is necessary to assert yourself and ask for a Yes or No Response, in order to understand clearly where the parent stands. Basically, this technique requires that you focus on any vague statement and clarify what you feel the parent is saying.

Parent: "Well, I don't know if I can do what you ask. I'll think about it."

Teacher: "I hear you saying you are not going to do what we discussed."

Parent: "Not really, I just, oh, well, I don't know."

Teacher: "It is vital for your son that we know where you stand, and if you will work with us. For his sake, we can't wait any longer. I need to know—Yes or No—if you will work with him at home?"

Parent: "Okay. Yes, I will. You can count on my support."

For very reluctant parents, it is helpful to write down their commitment, either positive or negative, and put it in their child's folder. It is even better if you can have the parents sign a "contract" indicating what they have committed themselves to do. When something is in writing and is signed, it adds a formality and significance to the commitment. This is the structure that some parents need.

Here is an edited excerpt from a conference in which the teacher used an assertive approach with a difficult parent. Note how the teacher clearly and firmly communicated the goals, objectives, rationale, and consequences. And, note how the teacher employed assertive communication skills.

Teacher: "I'm glad you could come today, Ms. C. As I told you on the phone, Fred is still having problems in relation to his academic work. He rarely completes any assignments. When he needs to be working, he sits and talks with his neighbors, or plays with small toys he brings from home. Here are some examples of his work from last week." (Documentation)

Parent: "None of these are even half finished!"

Teacher: "I know. That's why I asked you to come in. I need your cooperation in working out a solution to Fred's academic problems." (Goal)

Parent: "I can't believe that he's a problem at school! He's never been a problem at home. I mean never!"

Teacher: "I understand he's not a problem at home, but he has some problems at school that I need your cooperation with in order to be effective. (Broken Record) The reason I need your help is because it is in Fred's best interest that we cooperate to help him with his academic problems. Fred needs to know that we are working together to help him. Ms. C., you and your husband are the most important people in Fred's life. You have more influence over Fred than we at school ever could. Fred must know that we will not tolerate his disrupting rather than working!" (Rationale)

Parent: "I still can't believe he's a problem!"

Teacher: "I understand, but the point you need to remember is that Fred is not a 'bad' child. He can behave, and the closer we cooperate, the easier it will be to help Fred."

Parent: "What can I do?"

Teacher: "I feel the best way we can help Fred is with a plan I have used with other parents of students who have difficulty doing their work. Every day I will send a note. On the note I will indicate if Fred has completed his work or what work he has not completed. If he has not completed his work, I would want you to see that he does. If he has completed his work, I would want you to let him know how pleased you are, and maybe provide him with some special treat." (Objectives)

Parent: "That plan is fine except that both my husband and I work. When am I going to find time to see that he does his work? You don't realize how busy I am!"

Teacher: "I understand it is difficult, but we need to remember this. The consequence of our not working together is that Fred will fall farther behind academically. He is already one year behind in math and reading. If his behavior continues, he will soon be one and a half years behind!" (Consequences)

Parent: "It's really that bad, isn't it?"

Teacher: "He is behind, but if we work together we can help him."

Parent: "Well, I'll have to sit down with my husband. I hear what you are saying—we need to do something."

Teacher: "I want to be sure I was clear on the support I need from you. Could you tell me what you heard me say?" (Active Sending of Message)

Parent: "We have to get on Fred. When we get a note that says he didn't finish his work, we have to make sure that he does it at home. If we receive a note that says he did complete his work, we need to let him know that we like it. Well, I guess he's just not going to be watching T.V. for awhile."

Teacher: "What do you mean?"

Parent: "If Fred doesn't do his work, he's not going to watch T.V. until he finishes it at home."

Teacher: "How do you plan to let him know you like it when he gets a good note?"

Parent: "Ice cream, what else? He loves ice cream!"

Teacher: "It sounds excellent. I really appreciate your cooperation!"

Parent: "Look, he's my child and I need to do something. But let me tell you something—you are the first teacher that has ever been straight with me about Fred, and I appreciate it."

Teacher: "Thank you. One last thing. I'll talk to Fred tomorrow and let him know what we have decided, and I would appreciate your doing the same. And, I'll be in touch with you to let you know how things are going."

Parent: "Fine, I'll be looking forward to your first note."

ASKING PRINCIPALS FOR HELP

Let's be straight. The principal is your boss, and we are all uptight when it comes to dealing with our boss. But don't forget that principals are "people" first, and "principals" second. Therefore, you are *capable* of asserting yourself with a principal, as you would assert yourself with a parent, peer, or any other adult.

When asking the principal to assist you with a particular child and problem, it is necessary to utilize the same basic procedures as were outlined on how to work with parents.

1. *Assert yourself as soon as you see that there is, or may be, a situation with a child in which you will need the principal's support:*

    "Mr. S., Mark does not respond well to my limits and I think it may be necessary in the near future for me to ask you to help reinforce my limits with him."

2. *Know specifically what you would want the principal to do (Goals):*

"Mr. S., I need your cooperation in setting limits on Mark's fighting in class."

3. *Determine how you want the principal to help you.* You need to plan this before you meet with the principal, but you also need to be open to any of his ideas. (Objectives):

"Mr. S., I would like to send Mark to your office whenever he fights, and have you reinforce my authority."

4. *Explain why you want and need the principal's assistance.* (Rationale) (Don't apologize or belittle yourself.)

"Mr. S., I need your help because I do not have limit-setting consequences in my classroom which are effective in influencing Mark to choose to stop fighting. I feel Mark respects you and your authority, and that your limits can make a significant difference."

5. *Be straight with the principal as to what you feel will happen if you do not get his support.* (Consequences):

"Unless something is done, I do not feel I can continue to have Mark in my class. He is too disruptive and will hurt somebody in the near future."

The most beneficial assertive communication skill to use with a principal to whom you are having difficulty expressing your wants is the *Broken Record.*

Teacher: "Ms. K., I feel I need to suspend Teresa when she has a violent temper tantrum, as she disrupts the entire class. I would like your support in convincing the parents that this is an appropriate action. (Assertive Statement)

Principal: "Ms. C., I know Teresa is a problem, but isn't there anything else you can do?"

Teacher: "No, I feel I need to suspend her and I need your support in doing so."

Principal: "But, you know how upset her father will get. I can't stand dealing with that man."

Teacher: "I know he is difficult, but I still need your support in suspending Teresa." (Broken Record)

Principal: "You are sure there is nothing else that can be done, like sending her to the Special Education class?"

Teacher: "No, the class is full. I feel she needs to be suspended and I need your support." (Broken Record)

Principal: "I hear what you are saying. It will be hard for me, but I will give you all the support you need with her parents."

Teacher: "I realize it will be hard for you, and I truly appreciate your support. It will help make my job easier and really be of help in the long run for Teresa."

The use of assertive skills can, and will, maximize the impact you have on the interactions with parents and principals. But, by becoming more assertive, you are not necessarily guaranteed that you will always get what you want from them. The parents still may not follow through at home, or the principal still may not provide the support you would have liked. You, at least, can and should have the satisfaction of knowing that you did all you could to obtain the assistance needed for yourself and the child.

11

IN CONCLUSION:

ASSERTIVE DISCIPLINE
COMES DOWN TO
THE ISSUE OF CHOICE

The cornerstone of *Assertive Discipline* is the potential positive influence a teacher can have on the behavior of her students. A teacher's potential impact was aptly described by Dr. Hiam Ginott in relating his experiences as a teacher in *Between Teacher and Child.*

"I have come to a frightening conclusion. I am the decisive element in the classroom. It is my personal approach that creates the climate. It is my daily mood that makes the weather. As a teacher I possess tremendous power to make a child's life miserable or joyous. I can be a tool of torture or an instrument of inspiration. I can humiliate or humor, hurt or heal. In all situations it is my response that decides whether a crisis will be escalated or de-escalated, and a child humanized or de-humanized."

Hand in hand with influence goes *responsibility.* When a teacher accepts the consequences of her potential influence, she is accepting the responsibility to choose, or not to choose, to utilize this potential for the best interest of herself and her students. This point is of great significance, and we need to elaborate on it further.

An assertive teacher recognizes the responsibility she has to herself and the children. She knows she can assert herself and get her needs and the children's needs met. She knows she can have an impact on her classroom if she *chooses* to do so. An assertive teacher is thus confronted by countless choices.

Will she choose to put in the effort verbally to set limits with the disruptive children to influence them to choose to stop disrupting?

Will she choose to put in the effort verbally to support the appropriate behavior of the unmotivated children to influence them to choose to improve their behavior?

Will she choose to put forth the effort to prepare and plan appropriate follow-through efforts, be it limit-setting or positive?

Will she choose to put forth the effort to develop consistently assertive responses in her classroom?

Will she choose to maintain realistically positive expectations of her ability to have an impact on the children's behavior?

Will she choose to put forth the effort to ask assertively for the help she needs from the child's parents or principal?

Other teachers choose not to accept the reality of their potential influence. Thus, they are confronted with the following situations: they place themselves in a "powerless" position; they view themselves as a helpless "victim" at the mercy of their students, their parents, the principal and/or the school system; in general they also feel or verbalize comments such as:

"There's nothing I can do for the child, he's just too disturbed for me to handle."

"These kids are brats. They won't listen to a word I say. They are hopeless, no one can teach them."

"That mother is bizarre. No one can deal with her."

"My principal is so uptight. No one can stand him, he's no support at all to me."

Such teachers become the "complainers." They complain about everyone or everything that "victimizes" them. They end up blaming all of their problems on others, such as:

"If that child wasn't in my room everything would be just fine."

"My problems with the class began the day that girl transferred in from the other school."

"Those parents are the ones to blame, they destroy everything I do."

"I could handle the children if I had a different principal."

Such a passive response style does not allow the teacher to be in a position to get her needs met in her classroom. Therefore, all of the principles that have been discussed and described in this book will be useless to such teachers. They will naturally respond to the methods and techniques presented with the comment, "They won't work for me because . . . the kids I work with are too rough, or the parents won't back me up, etc." It is, again, their choice to take this position; and they have to live with the consequences of their choice.

An assertive teacher also has to deal with the consequences of her choices. But she is in a position to change her choices if the consequences she is receiving do not meet her needs. Here are some examples of what we mean.

A teacher was confronted by a child who would fight constantly in class. By the end of each day the teacher had a headache from dealing with his disruptions. She felt that suspending him would motivate him to stop fighting, but she did not do so for she felt it was "too severe a punishment." She initially thus chose not to assert herself, and the consequence of her behavior was that the child continued to fight and she continued to have headaches. When she finally got fed up with the fighting and the headaches, she chose to assert herself and suspended the child each and every time he had a fight. The consequences of her choice were that the boy stopped fighting and she stopped having headaches.

Another teacher had a highly disruptive child in her class who would clamor for attention in any way possible, be it running around the room, leaving the room, or yelling out. The constant limit-setting with the child wore the teacher out. She knew the child obviously needed more positive support and attention, but she initially felt she didn't have the extra time to spend with the child. Thus, at first she chose not to assert herself and had to deal with the consequence, her being worn out from dealing with the child's constant disruptions. After a few weeks, the teacher finally got fed up and chose to assert herself. She arranged to provide the child free time with her, if the child remained in his seat and did not shout out. The consequences for her choice were less hassles for her, as the child's behavior noticeably improved.

A new teacher was confronted with a difficult class of numerous children with behavior problems. Her inability to deal with the problems was causing her complete frustration. She knew she had to put more time into planning how she would deal assertively with the problems; but she felt since she was new, she had to put all of her time into planning her lessons. She thus chose initially not to assert herself. The consequences were she remained frustrated, as the children continued to disrupt. She finally came to the realization that the time put into planning lessons was wasted because the class was so disruptive that minimal time actually went into academic work. She then chose to sit down each night and work up a daily discipline plan which would enable her to deal assertively with the children's disruptive behavior. The consequences of her choice were a better behaved class and less frustrations.

A teacher had a tall, hostile boy who would frequently talk back to her. She would become very upset at his verbal abuse, which she didn't feel she could handle without assistance. She knew she needed the principal's assistance, but was afraid of what he might think of her if she asked for help. She thus chose at first not to assert herself and suffered the consequences of having to put up with the child's verbal abuse. Finally, one day he cussed at her and she decided it was time to assert herself. She chose to ask the principal to assist her in dealing with the boy. It was arranged that the boy would go immediately to the principal's office whenever he talked back to her. The consequence of her choice was that the boy stopped his verbal abuse and she was less upset.

Your use of *Assertive Discipline*, thus, comes down to the issue of choice. Will you choose to take responsibility for your potential influence? Will you choose to utilize your potential for the best interest of yourself and the children?

We have positive expectations. We feel you will!

ASSERTIVE DISCIPLINE WORKSHEETS

ROADBLOCKS TO ASSERTIVENESS WORKSHEET

Which students have you felt had specific problems which prevented you from being able to influence their behavior? List both the students and their problems.

1. _____   4. _____

2. _____   5. _____

3. _____   6. _____

With which students have you failed to set sufficiently firm consistent limits?

1. _____   4. _____

2. _____   5. _____

3. _____   6. _____

With which students, if any, have you failed to set firm limits for fear they might not like you, or school?

1. _____   3. _____

2. _____   4. _____

With which students, if any, have you failed to set firm limits for fear that the limits may cause an already troubled child further undue stress or problems?

1. _____   3. _____

2. _____   4. _____

With which students, if any, do you fail to set firm limits out of fear of your inability to handle their possible reactions, outbursts, tantrums, crying, etc.?

1. _____   3. _____

2. _____   4. _____

With which students, if any, do you fail to set firm limits because of the reality that you need additional support from the parents in order to be effective?

1. _____   3. _____

2. _____   4. _____

With which students, if any, do you fail to provide the additional incentives necessary to motivate their appropriate behavior?

1. _____   3. _____

2. _____   4. _____

YOUR WANTS AND NEEDS WORKSHEET

List the five behaviors you want and need from your students to function at your maximum potential.

1. _____
2. _____
3. _____
4. _____
5. _____

What activity periods (quiet, work, etc.) do you utilize with your class? What behaviors do you want and need for each activity period?

Activity Period _____   Activity Period _____

1. _____   1. _____
2. _____   2. _____
3. _____   3. _____

Activity Period _____   Activity Period _____

1. _____   1. _____
2. _____   2. _____
3. _____   3. _____

Activity Period _____   Activity Period _____

1. _____   1. _____
2. _____   2. _____
3. _____   3. _____

Analyze your general response style according to the following criteria:

1. Do you assertively communicate, verbally and non-verbally, the behaviors you want for your students?

_____

_____

_____

2. In general, how do you verbally respond to the student's behavior that you do not want (Verbal Limit-Setting)—assertively, non-assertively, or hostilely? If you feel that you respond assertively, do your responses influence the students to eliminate their inappropriate behavior?

_____

_____

_____

3. In general, how do you verbally respond to the students' behavior that you do want (Positive Verbal Assertions)—assertively, non-assertively, or hostilely?

_____

_____

_____

4. When necessary, how do you generally follow-through on your limit-setting demands—assertively, non-assertively, or hostilely? If you feel you respond "assertively," do your responses maximize your po-

tential to influence the students' behavior, in order
to eliminate that which is inappropriate? _____

_____

_____

5. When necessary, how do you generally follow-
through on your positive verbal assertions—assertively, non-assertively, or hostilely? If you feel you
are "assertive," does your response maximize your
potential influence on the child and increase his appropriate behavior? _____

_____

6. How effectively do you plan your discipline efforts? _____

_____

7. Review your self-analysis. What changes do you
need to engage in to increase your effectiveness in
meeting your needs?

1. _____

2. _____

3. _____

4. _____

If you have specific "powerful children" whom you
are having difficulty dealing with, respond again to

the 7 questions, but this time in relation to your response style with these children.

Child's Name: _____

1. Communication of wants and needs: _____
   _____

2. Verbal Limit-Setting: _____
   _____

3. Positive Assertions: _____
   _____

4. Limit-Setting Follow-Through: _____
   _____

5. Positive Assertion Follow-Through: _____
   _____

6. Planning Discipline: _____
   _____

7. Review Changes:
   1. _____
   2. _____
   3. _____
   4. _____

POSITIVE ASSERTION
FOLLOW-THROUGH SURVEY

Child's Name _____ Date _____

This survey should be filled out in the presence of the student. Ask each question of the student. The student's responses will assist you in determining appropriate positive follow-through consequences that will motivate the student.

1. If you did a good job at school who would you like me to tell? _____

2. What adult (teacher, aide, counselor etc.) would you like to earn time with? _____

3. What classmate would you like to earn more time with? _____

4. What is your favorite activity at school? _____

_____

5. What activity would you like to do more often?

_____

6. What special privilege would you like to earn?

_____

7. What is the best reward I could give you at school?

_____

ASSERTIVE DISCIPLINE PLAN WORKSHEET

Discipline problem to be worked on (briefly describe)

_____

_____

Behaviors you want: 1. _____

                                 2. _____

                                 3. _____

Behaviors you don't want: 1. _____

                                 2. _____

                                 3. _____

Limit-setting follow-through consequences you will utilize: _____

_____

_____

Planning you will need to engage in to implement the consequences: _____

_____

_____

Positive follow-through consequences you will utilize: _____

_____

_____

Planning you will need to engage in to implement
the consequences: _____

_____

_____

Remember the Key Principles of Planning
1) Don't assume the behaviors of others (principal,
   parents etc.)
2) Anticipate all possible problems that might hinder your follow-through efforts
3) Leave nothing to doubt
4) Don't meet with the student(s) until your follow-
   through plan is ready

TEACHER-PARENT CONFERENCE
WORKSHEET

Child's Name _____ Date _____

Mother's Name _____

Father's Name _____

Goal(s) For Conference: "I need your cooperation at home with your child's behavior" etc.

1. _____

_____

2. _____

_____

Objectives For Conference: What Do You Specifically Want or Need The Parents To Do. i.e. Reward or Punish at home.

1. _____

2. _____

3. _____

Rationale: Why Are You Asking Parents To Do It?

_____

_____

_____

Consequences: What You Feel Will Happen To The
Child If The Parents Do Not Act.

Documentation: What Factual Evidence Do You
Have To Back Up Your Assertions?

TEACHER-PRINCIPAL DISCIPLINE WORKSHEET

Briefly describe the discipline problem you need assistance with (include a description of what you have already attempted to do, and documentation of the problem)

_____

_____

_____

_____

What do you want from your principal? (goal)

_____

What do you specifically want your principal to do? (objectives)

_____

_____

Why do you need your principal's assistance? (rationale)

_____

_____

What do you feel will occur if your principal does not provide you support with this problem? (consequences)

_____

_____

Materials for Teachers

ASSERTIVE DISCIPLINE®

Prod. #	Item Description	Unit Price
CA1009	Assertive Discipline for Parents	$ 7.95
CA1010	Parent Resource Guide	7.95
CA1016	Assertive Discipline Text	7.95
CA1019	Resource Materials Workbook, Gr. 7-12	7.95
CA1024	Resource Materials Workbook, Gr. K-6	7.95
CA1026	Teacher's Mailbox	5.95
CA1029	Back to School with Assertive Discipline	9.95
CA1033	Desktop Motivators, Gr. 1-4	4.95
CA1034	Awards for Reinforcing Positive Behavior, Gr. 1-3	4.95
CA1035	Awards for Reinforcing Positive Behavior, Gr. 4-6	4.95
CA1036	Summer Motivators	4.95
CA1037	Fall Motivators	4.95
CA1038	Winter Motivators	4.95
CA1039	Spring Motivators	4.95
CA1040	Assertive Discipline Teacher Kit, Gr. K-6	59.95
CA1041	Assertive Discipline Teacher Kit, Gr. 7-12	59.95
CA1042	Bulletin Boards for Reinf. Positive Behav., Gr. K-3	7.95
CA1043	Bulletin Boards for Reinf. Positive Behav., Gr. 4-7	7.95
CA1048	Positive Reinforcement Activities, Gr. K-6	5.95
CA1049	Parent Conference Book	6.95
CA1052	Positive Reinforcement Activities, Gr. 7-12	5.95
CA1053	Schoolwide Positive Activities	8.95
CA1063	Teacher's Plan Book Plus #2	4.95
CA1064	Teacher's Plan Book Plus #1	4.95
CA1071	Wanted for Good Behavior Poster	3.50
CA1072	Star Tracks Positive Reinforcement Poster, Gr. 4-6	3.50
CA1073	Classroom Rules Poster, Gr. 1-3	2.25
CA1074	Classroom Rules Poster, Gr. 4-12	2.25
CA1075	We're on the Right Track Pos. Reinf. Poster, Gr. 1-3	3.50
CA1076	Marbles-in-a-Jar Poster (incl. 150 marble stickers)	4.95

Assertive Discipline Inservice Workshops   A Lee Canter consultant will travel to your district to train staff, support staff or parents in the skills to solve behavior problems. For information contact our office.